15,-

MANON BELLET
L'ONDE
D'UNE OMBRE

Kunstmuseum Solothurn

Musée Jenisch Vevey

8 L'EFFET « CHARLOTTE »
THE "CHARLOTTE" EFFECT
Julie Enckell Julliard

36 SCHATTENBILDER
SHADOW PICTURES
Patricia Bieder

72 **IDEAS IN PROCESS**
Stéphanie Serra

88 JOUER AVEC LE FEU
Manon Bellet en conversation avec
Mathieu Copeland
PLAYING WITH FIRE
Manon Bellet in conversation with
Mathieu Copeland

114 **APPENDIX**

◄◄ SANS TITRE SANS ENCRE
2010, DETAILS

Das Kunstmuseum Solothurn setzt sich seit Jahren konsequent für das Schaffen von Schweizer Kunstschaffenden ein. Ein besonderes Interesse gilt dabei der Vermittlung von Arbeiten auf Papier. Diese nehmen im Werk von Manon Bellet (*1979) nicht nur einen besonderen Platz ein, sie zeigen sich auch in sehr eigenständiger und zeitgemässer Form. Mit ihren komplexen Arbeiten ermöglicht die Künstlerin eine existenzielle Erörterung von grosser Intensität. Es freut uns daher sehr, diese erste museale Einzelausstellung initiieren zu dürfen.

Die Partnerschaft mit dem Musée Jenisch Vevey ist ebenso erfreulich wie naheliegend: Mit dem Medium der Zeichnung teilen wir nicht nur dieselbe Leidenschaft, mit dem Musée Jenisch Vevey konnte zugleich die Heimatregion der Künstlerin angesprochen werden. Unser erster Dank gebührt Manon Bellet, die sich dem Ausstellungs- und Buchprojekt mit grosser Ernsthaftigkeit zugewendet hat. Danken möchten wir auch der Direktorin des Musée Jenisch Vevey, Julie Enckell Julliard und ihrer stellvertretenden Kuratorin Stéphanie Serra für die intensive Zusammenarbeit. Die Grafikerin und Verlegerin Anja Lutz hat sich engagiert mit Manon Bellets Schaffen beschäftigt und dafür eine stimmige Buchform gefunden. Schliesslich danken wir unserem ganzen Museumsteam, das sich für das gute Gelingen der Ausstellung eingesetzt hat.

Christoph Vögele, Konservator Kunstmuseum Solothurn
Patricia Bieder, Kuratorin der Ausstellung

Une fois par an, le Musée Jenisch Vevey accueille un ou une jeune artiste, pour une première exposition muséale assortie d'une première monographie. Deuxième musée d'art du canton de Vaud, le Jenisch privilégie les artistes travaillant librement le dessin, l'estampe ou la matière papier, dans des interventions souvent créées *in situ*.

Née à Vevey, Manon Bellet place depuis plusieurs années le papier au cœur de son travail. Disloquée, brûlée, altérée, chauffée, la page se transforme sous l'impulsion de l'artiste qui explore, ainsi, ses nouvelles vies possibles. Manon Bellet propose ici un projet en deux volets, qu'elle décline de Soleure à Vevey. Dans une trajectoire tracée «à rebours», reliant la Suisse alémanique où elle a longtemps vécu (à Bâle en particulier), à la région de ses origines (la Riviera vaudoise), l'artiste trouve le moyen de jeter un regard transversal sur son parcours. Je remercie chaleureusement Manon Bellet pour notre belle collaboration. Ma vive reconnaissance s'adresse au Kunstmuseum Solothurn et à Christoph Vögele, pour avoir rendu possible le partenariat entre nos deux institutions. Ma gratitude va enfin vers celles qui ont œuvré pour que le projet prenne corps: Patricia Bieder, commissaire de l'exposition de Soleure, Stéphanie Serra, conservatrice adjointe au Musée Jenisch et Anja Lutz, éditrice et graphiste du livre.

Julie Enckell Julliard, Directrice, Musée Jenisch Vevey

L'EFFET « CHARLOTTE »

Julie Enckell Julliard

THE "CHARLOTTE" EFFECT

Julie Enckell Julliard

L'index est pointé sur l'iris. À mesure que le doigt s'en approche, l'œil se meut, en saccades, comme pour échapper à une trop grande proximité. Par intermittence, la paupière se clôt, protège la pupille du contact de la main, désormais si proche de la cornée. Baigné d'une lumière rouge, *Charlotte* (2004) est un film au cadre resserré et dense, qui raconte l'effet indirect d'un geste à la fois transgressif et sensuel. Pour Steve McQueen (*1969), son auteur, « l'œil est la seule partie du corps qui concerne autant l'intérieur. Une blessure ouverte »[1] : la main de l'artiste guide dans ses mouvements, sans même le toucher, l'iris de Charlotte Rampling, faisant de sa célèbre paupière la principale protagoniste de son œuvre.

Dans le quartier de Wedding au nord de Berlin, l'atelier de Manon Bellet, née à Vevey en 1979, est aussi lumineux qu'épuré : quelques pages épinglées sur un mur blanc, une table recouverte de vieux polaroids récupérés et altérés par le temps (*In the Corner of Your Memory*, 2012–2013, pp. 110–113). Sur un petit bureau, à côté de l'ordinateur, une pile de cahiers noirs remplis d'annotations, de fragments de textes retranscrits ou d'esquisses. La zone la plus chargée dans cet espace est certainement celle que l'artiste nomme le « labo ». C'est là, à droite en entrant, que se concentre la part la plus expérimentale et prospective de son travail : on remarque, sur la table, des aimants, de la limaille de fer, un impressionnant bloc de graphite, des essais de frottages sur papier d'architecte, etc. Au mur, quelques feuilles d'un papier très fin maculées de poudre métallique et des petits branchages asséchés. Plus bas, une série

The index finger extends towards the iris. As the finger draws closer, the eye moves, twitchily, as if to prevent it from coming too near. Intermittently, the eyelid shuts, protecting the pupil from contact with the hand which is now so close to the cornea. Suffused with red light, *Charlotte* (2004) is a film with a tight, dense frame which recounts the indirect effect of a gesture that is at once transgressive and sensual. For the English artist Steve McQueen (*1969), its author, "the eye is the only part of the body that is all about the inside as such. Like an open wound."[1] The eye whose movements the artist's hand guides without even touching it is that of Charlotte Rampling; her famous eyelid the chief protagonist of his work.

In the Wedding district of northern Berlin, the studio of Manon Bellet, born in Vevey in 1979, is as light as it is uncluttered: a few pages pinned to a white wall, a table covered with old, rescued Polaroids faded by time (*In the Corner of Your Memory,* 2012–2013, pp. 110–113). On a small desk, beside the computer, a pile of black notebooks filled with annotations, retranscribed fragments of texts, and sketches. The most charged area of this space is undoubtedly what the artist refers to as the "lab." It is here, on the right as one enters the room, that we find the most experimental and prospective part of

de curieux petits objets saillants aux formes organiques, formés par de la limaille agglutinée de manière aléatoire autour d'un aimant. Enfin, seule tache rouge au milieu de cet accrochage presque uniformément minéral, une carte postale reproduisant un *still* de *Charlotte*. De la grande rétrospective de Steve McQueen présentée au Schaulager de Bâle à l'été 2013, Manon Bellet a rapporté ce souvenir, avant de l'inclure dans la sphère intime de l'atelier. « L'artiste ne touche jamais l'œil, il ne fait que déclencher le mouvement »[2] : ce qui importe ici, c'est le fait que McQueen génère d'abord une réaction, qu'il n'ait pas directement prise sur les mouvements rétiniens. Le film rend compte des états que le geste de l'artiste engendre, avec toute la part de hasard que la situation peut comprendre. Dans l'atelier berlinois de Manon Bellet, *Charlotte* manifeste cette manière particulière d'aborder la création artistique : animer la matière plutôt que la manipuler, déclencher plutôt que contrôler, transformer plutôt que produire. Celle qui cherche surtout à « révéler ce qui existe déjà » fait d'abord éprouver des vies nouvelles aux matériaux. Trouvés ou récupérés, parfois obsolètes, ceux-ci sont le plus souvent peu sophistiqués. Ils sont choisis pour leur vulnérabilité et leur capacité de transformation. Aussi le papier, sous toutes ses formes – papier thermique, papier fax ou carbone, papier de soie – figure-t-il au cœur de l'attention de Manon Bellet. Plus il est fin et frêle, plus il est susceptible de se marquer et de s'altérer, de conserver la trace d'une expérience sensible. Souvent volatiles ou translucides, ce sont les plus réactifs qui retiennent en

her work: on the table, we can make out magnets, iron filings, an impressive block of graphite, experiments in rubbing on architect's paper, etc. On the wall are some sheets of very fine paper smudged with metal powder and little dried branches. Lower down, a series of curious small objects, organic in form, created by the filings gathered randomly around a magnet. Finally, the solitary red patch in the middle of this almost exclusively mineral assemblage: a postcard depicting a still from *Charlotte*. Manon Bellet brought this souvenir back from the major Steve McQueen retrospective at the Schaulager in Basel in summer 2013, and has now incorporated it into the intimate sphere of the studio. "The artist never touches the eye, he merely prompts the movement"[2]: what matters here is that McQueen begins by eliciting a reaction, without exerting any direct control over the movements of the retina. The film thus gives an account of the states that the artist's gesture engenders, with all the element of chance that the situation can involve. In Manon Bellet's Berlin studio, *Charlotte* bears witness to this particular way of approaching artistic creation: animating the material rather than manipulating, initiating rather than controlling, transforming rather than producing. Manon Bellet, who seeks above all to "reveal what already exists" first allows the materials to experience new lives.

ATELIER BERLIN
2013

Found or rescued, sometimes obsolete, they are mostly quite unsophisticated. They are chosen for their vulnerability and their capacity for transformation. Thus paper, in all its forms – thermal paper, fax or carbon paper, tissue paper – attracts Manon Bellet's closest attention. The finer and frailer it is, the more it is susceptible to marking and to change, to conserving the trace of a felt experience. The papers are often volatile or translucent; it is the most reactive among them that interest her most. We only need to think about the video *Vestiges* (2010, pp. 20–22), in which we see a book without text, its pages bathed in light and moving from mere contact with the air. Or the series of cyanotypes entitled *Sous sur face* (2012–2013, pp. 47–52, 55), a series of salvaged, translucent plastic bags reminiscent of beings *in utero.* Or indeed the various thermal papers, which can transform themselves or react on contact with the heat that the artist uses. Take for example the *Imagerie du hasard* (2011–2012, pp. 30–35), a series of fax papers retracing the history of its progressive blackening as it comes into contact with a previously heated metal plate. For the "croquis de chaleur" (2012–2013, pp. 64–71), produced at the beginning of the attempt to put thought into motion, Manon Bellet uses a heated metal tip on heat-sensitive paper. Here it is the heat that determines the mark left on the image medium,

particulier l'attention de l'artiste. Il suffit de penser au film *Vestiges* (2010, pp. 20–22), où un livre sans texte, aux pages traversées de lumière, voit celles-ci se mouvoir au seul contact de l'air. Ou à la suite de cyanotypes *Sous sur face* (2012–2013, pp. 47–52, 55), présentant à la manière d'êtres *in utero* une série de sacs plastiques translucides récupérés. Ou encore aux différents papiers thermiques, capables de se transformer ou de réagir au contact de la chaleur, que l'artiste utilise. C'est aussi le cas pour les *Imagerie du hasard* (2011–2012, pp. 30–35), suite de papiers fax retraçant l'histoire de son noircissement progressif au contact de d'une plaque de métal préalablement chauffée. Pour les « croquis de chaleur » (2012–2013, pp. 64–71), réalisés en amont du travail comme une mise en mouvement de la pensée, Manon Bellet travaille enfin en intervenant avec une pointe métallique chauffée sur un papier thermosensible. C'est ici la chaleur qui conditionne la trace sur le support, elle qui fixe le temps possible de l'empreinte. L'expérience ne dure que quelques instants, jusqu'à ce que la température de l'outil diminue et n'ait plus d'impact sur le papier.

La vulnérabilité des matériaux induit ainsi, nécessairement, une certaine impermanence des œuvres. Le changement, la mobilité, même infime, devient une condition fondamentale de la création, ce qui fait que l'œuvre existe. Une pliure à peine perceptible du papier, sa palpitation au contact de l'air : l'accent se pose sur ces menues nuances qui animent la matière et la font vibrer. Dans le travail de Manon Bellet, les images ne se fixent donc pas, la matière n'est

dictating the time available for the imprint to be made. The experiment lasts but a few seconds, until the instrument begins to cool and no longer has any effect on the paper.

The vulnerability of the materials thus inevitably gives the works a measure of impermanence. Change, motion – however small – in fact becomes a fundamental condition of creation: it is what makes the work exist. An almost imperceptible creasing of the paper, a fluttering in the breeze: the emphasis is on these minor nuances that animate the material and make it vibrate. In the work of Manon Bellet, then, images are not fixed, the material has never come to a stop; it always contains the potential for a new life. The installations *Burning Air* (2010/13, pp. 17–19) and *Brève braise* (2011, pp. 58–59) consist of charred, dislocated papers on walls. Here, curiously, their progressive disintegration through contact with the air, the tattered remnants falling to the floor, expresses not an ultimate form of destruction, but rather the stirring of a new energy, slow and silent. In this universe, almost entirely black and white, the material thus harbours a continuing vitality, an imperceptible movement, an infinite reactivity.

Never truly settling, the work now encompasses an adopted form of randomness or potential failure (cf. *Playing*

jamais arrêtée. Les installations *Burning Air* (2010/13, pp. 17–19) ou *Brève braise* (2011, pp. 58–59) présentent au mur des papiers calcinés et disloqués. Etrangement, leur démantèlement progressif au contact de l'air, la chute des lambeaux au sol n'expriment pas ici une ultime forme de destruction, mais le frémissement d'une nouvelle énergie lente et silencieuse. Dans cet univers presque unilatéralement noir et blanc, la matière connaît ainsi une vitalité continue, un imperceptible mouvement, une réactivité infinie.

Sans jamais réellement se fixer, l'œuvre comprend dès lors une forme assumée d'aléatoire ou d'échec potentiel (cf. *Jouer avec le feu. Manon Bellet en conversation avec Mathieu Copeland,* p. 88). Cultivant cette ouverture au hasard, réfutant l'entière maîtrise plastique dont elle pourrait se prévaloir, Manon Bellet recherche et entretient une poétique des failles ou de la fragilité, qu'elle allie, toujours, à une mise en retrait du geste. Avec *Vestiges,* le livre sans texte aux pages opalescentes voit celles-ci se mouvoir au contact de l'air : rien de calculé dans le balancement des feuilles translucides ; un mouvement aléatoire seulement, nous ramenant, au travers de la symbolique de l'objet, à la précarité de l'existence et au passage du temps. Ailleurs, le papier fax, placé au contact de plaques de métal chauffées, s'assombrit pour revêtir l'aspect d'anciens clichés de paysages anonymes et aériens (*Imagerie du hasard*) ; l'œuvre prend la forme de papiers de soie calcinés qui s'étiolent et s'amoncellent sur le sol sous l'impulsion de l'air (*Burning Air* ou *Brève braise*). La calcination du papier renvoie

PIPER AT THE GATES OF DAWN
2012

certes, dans ce dernier cas, à une forme irréversible d'inertie, mais l'œuvre de Manon Bellet lui garantit, paradoxalement, une existence à laquelle on ne saurait mettre un terme. Comme si les travaux ne pouvaient échapper à la continuelle épreuve du temps et de l'espace : au moment de leur mise en exposition, les rouleaux de papier fax de *Sans titre sans encre* (2010, pp. 2–4, 102, 104–105) commencent ainsi leur lente altération au contact des radiateurs. Formant au mur un disque de papier de soie calciné, *Brève braise* rejoue, le temps de sa présentation au public, le caractère instable de l'existence en se décomposant, progressivement, au fil du passage des visiteurs.

Faisant de la libre évolution de la matière un facteur clé de ses créations, Manon Bellet cultive donc une forme de retrait. Elle nourrit même, pour ses œuvres, le rêve d'une vie autarcique, d'un devenir autonome, qu'il ne s'agirait que de valoriser et d'observer. Dans la perspective de ce lâcher-prise, l'évolution plastique des matériaux est soumise aux énergies environnantes: l'air, la chaleur ou les courants électriques ou magnétiques, celles-ci sont le plus souvent, invisibles et discrètes. Ce sont elles qui animent les matières choisies, elles qui parviennent à les transformer. Se limitant à déclencher l'action, Manon Bellet s'en remet à ces forces, souvent impalpables ou imperceptibles à l'œil nu. L'air joue ainsi un rôle clé, dans *Vestiges* ou *Burning Air,* tandis que c'est la chaleur qui conditionne le devenir plastique des *Burning Lines* (2010–2011, pp. 62–63) ou des *Imagerie du hasard*. Ces facteurs sont parfois déterminants

with Fire. Manon Bellet in conversation with Mathieu Copeland, p. 88). Cultivating this openness to chance, refusing to impose the full sculptural mastery that she could assert, Manon Bellet searches for and maintains a poetry of flaws or fragility, where the gesture is invariably relegated to the background. With *Vestiges* – the blank book, its pages bathed in light and moving in the breeze – there is nothing calculated in the back-and-forth movement of the translucent pages; there is merely random motion, reminding us, through the symbolism of the object, of the precariousness of existence and the passage of time. The fax paper darkens when it comes into contact with the heated metal plates, coming to resemble old photographs of anonymous landscapes from the air *(Imagerie du hasard)*; the work takes the form of burnt tissue paper wilting and disintegrating on the ground upon contact with the air (*Burning Air* or *Brève braise*). Unquestionably, in the latter case, the charring of the paper suggests an irreversible form of inertia; but the work of Manon Bellet paradoxically guarantees it an existence which one would not dream of bringing to an end. It is as if these works were unable to escape a continual test of time and space: as soon as they are put on display, the rolls of fax paper in *Sans titre sans encre* (2010, pp. 2–4, 102, 104–105) thus begin their slow deterioration through exposure to

pour la composition même d'une pièce : dans *Piper at the Gates of Dawn* (2012, p. 14) l'électricité statique permet la convergence des lambeaux de papiers de soie brûlés sur le premier vinyle des Pink Floyd. L'afflux du papier disloqué sur le support fait ici écho au conte de Grimm dont est issu le titre de l'album, où le fifre Hamelin parvient à susciter la confluence des rats hors de la ville par son chant. Dans les cahiers noirs, de petits aimants se fixent au dos des pages comprenant la trace du passage du métal. Ailleurs, l'attraction de l'aimant configure littéralement les petites sculptures de limaille : accroché au mur, il est le point de confluence de la matière volatile que l'artiste fait pleuvoir à sa proximité.

Qu'il s'agisse de celle du cahier ou de la paroi de l'atelier, la force magnétique a pour vertu d'inscrire la matière, aussi fragile qu'elle soit, dans une certaine spatialité. Bien que très organique dans ses contours, la sculpture en limaille n'en possède pas moins des accents telluriques. Elle nous rappelle que l'œuvre de Manon Bellet a pour caractéristique de marier la matière fugace à une sorte d'ancrage. Un ancrage relevant, avant tout, de l'expérience dont les objets conservent la mémoire ou la trace. Il ne s'agit jamais ici de mettre en scène les effets des énergies convoquées, mais d'en induire plutôt la présence ou le passage, de manière à marquer une transformation ou un mouvement. Lorsque dans *Vestiges* le papier translucide se soulève, le changement se situe au niveau du plus petit détail. Il consiste en une digression minime, en un écart différentiel à peine perceptible avec l'état de la matière trouvée. À

the radiators. Forming a disk of burnt tissue paper on the wall, *Brève braise* replays the time of its presentation to the public, the unstable character of existence, gradually decomposing as visitors pass by it.

By making the unimpeded evolution of the material a key factor in her creations, Manon Bellet thus practises a form of self-effacement. She even nurtures the dream of an independent life for her works, an autonomous becoming that asks only to be appreciated and observed. In this process of letting go, the materials change their form in response to the energies that surround them. The air, the heat, the electric or magnetic currents, are mostly invisible and discreet. It is they that animate the chosen materials and transform them. Content merely to initiate the action, Manon Bellet hands over control to these forces, which are often impalpable or imperceptible to the naked eye. The air thus plays a central role in *Vestiges* or *Burning Air,* while in the *Burning Lines* (2010–2011, pp. 62–63) or *Imagerie du hasard* it is the heat that determines the future form. These factors sometimes dictate the very composition of a piece: in *Piper at the Gates of Dawn* (2012, p. 14), static electricity causes the scraps of burnt tissue paper to converge on the first album by Pink Floyd. The flow of the dismembered paper towards the substrate here recalls the Grimm's fairy tale from which the

BURNING AIR
2010

BURNING AIR
2010, DETAIL

album takes its title, and in which the Pied Piper of Hamelin draws the rats away from the town by playing his tune. In the black notebooks, tiny magnets are attached to the reverse of the pages containing the trace of the metal's passage. Elsewhere, the attraction of the magnet literally configures the little sculptures of iron filings: attached to the wall, it is the point at which the volatile material gathers, as the artist scatters it from close by.

Whether in the notebook or on the wall of the studio, the magnetic force has the virtue of endowing the material, however fragile it may be, with a certain spatiality. Although highly organic in its contours, the iron filing sculpture nevertheless suggests the work of earthly currents. It reminds us that the work of Manon Bellet is characterised by the combination of the fleeting material with a kind of anchorage: an anchorage that, above all, derives from the experience whose memory or traces the objects retain. The aim is never to dramatise the effects of the energies that have been summoned up, but rather to induce their presence or passage, so as to mark a transformation or a movement. When the translucent paper in *Vestiges* is lifted up, the change takes place at the level of the smallest detail. It is a minute digression, a differential, barely perceptible separation from the state of the found material. Inspired by the scene staged in *Charlotte,* the works

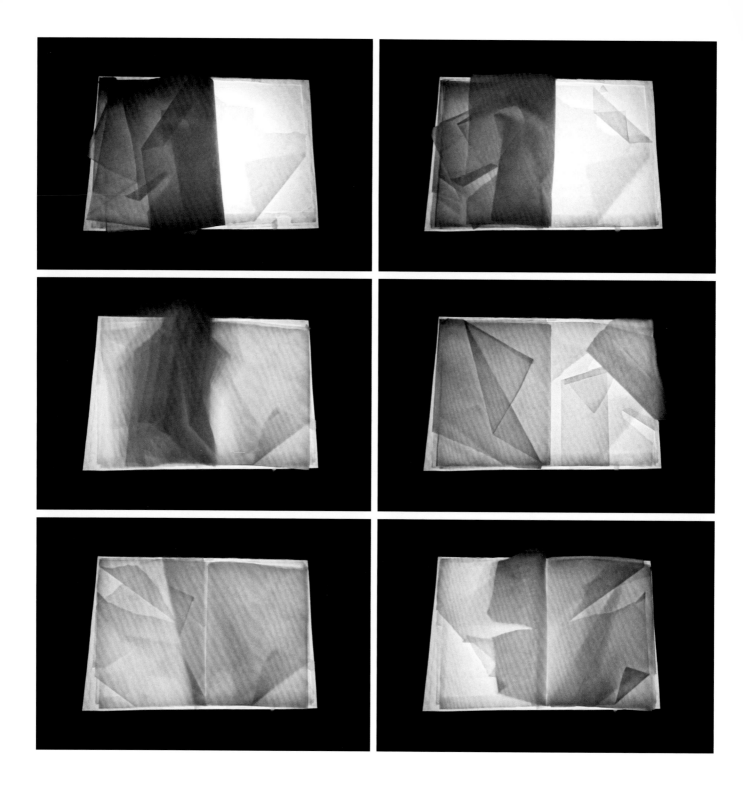

l'instar de ce que *Charlotte* met en scène, les œuvres de Manon Bellet existent ainsi dans leurs infimes nuances. Elles nous plongent dans les dimensions infinitésimales de l'expérience.

Dans la lignée de ce qui pour Marcel Duchamp (1887–1968) relevait de l'*infra-mince*[3], Manon Bellet privilégie l'action différée à l'effet immédiat, la circulation silencieuse aux effets tonitruants. Il faut se souvenir ici de ce dessaisissement du geste ayant conduit Duchamp au ready-made. De sa manière de limiter l'intention artistique au fait de ne marquer qu'une infime différence, d'effectuer ce déplacement susceptible de rendre une situation altérée ou enrichie sémantiquement. C'est ainsi que pour *Piston de courant d'air* (1914), l'artiste ne fait que marquer un seuil, une séparation, en plaçant une résille devant une fenêtre. Avec *Air de Paris* (1919), la frontière prend la forme d'un flacon. Il faudrait poursuivre la comparaison et dire combien la perception du temps rejoint chez Manon Bellet celle de l'inventeur du ready-made. Combien l'effet différé joue un rôle dans son travail, qui ne se fige pas, comme nous l'avons vu, au seuil de l'espace d'exposition. Ici l'attention ne se porte pas sur le résultat ou l'aboutissement, mais sur le passage du temps, sur le moment de l'élaboration. Manon Bellet a souvent privilégié, à ce titre, les procédés au long cours. Par leur dimension artisanale, ils font place au hasard et à l'étonnement. Elle apprécie l'espace du laboratoire, où elle a expérimenté adolescente des tirages photographiques, mais aussi celui de l'atelier de gravure, découvert lors de sa formation à l'Ecole cantonale d'art

of Manon Bellet also exist in their tiniest nuances. They immerse us in the infinitesimal dimensions of experience. Drawing on what Marcel Duchamp (1887–1968) identified as the *infra-mince* [infra-thin],[3] Manon Bellet favours deferred action over immediate impact, silent circulation over dramatic effects. It was, after all, a withdrawal from the gesture that led Duchamp to the ready-made: it was his way of limiting artistic intention to the mere signalling of a minute difference, effecting a displacement that could render a situation semantically altered or enriched. In *Piston de courant d'air* (1914), for example, the artist simply marks a threshold, a separation, by placing a fishnet in front of a window. In *Air de Paris* (1919), the frontier takes the form of an ampoule. We may continue this comparison and note how the perception of time in Manon Bellet harks back to the inventor of the ready-made: how the deferred effect plays a role in her work which, as we have seen, does not settle on the threshold of the exhibition space. Here, the attention is focused not on the result or the culmination, but on the passage of time, on the moment of elaboration. To this end, Manon Bellet has often favoured long-drawn out processes. Through their artisanship, they create space for chance and wonder. She values the space of the laboratory in which she conducted her teenage experiments in printing

du Valais. En dépit du fait que les œuvres traduisent souvent des instants fugaces, la durée du processus est ainsi conditionnelle de la création. Même si, paradoxalement, bon nombre des travaux de Manon Bellet se définissent par la perte ou l'absence, s'ils se trament en négatif. Dans l'économie des moyens mis en œuvre, les pièces *n'ajoutent* donc pas, ou très peu. Elles portent leur attention sur un mouvement infime, sur un « presque rien », qu'elles mettent en contact avec les forces les plus impalpables pour susciter une simple nuance. Dans les *Imagerie du hasard,* comme dans ses tout premiers travaux effectués à même le mur au stylo effaceur, la disparition de l'état originel du support engendre la composition. Dans la suite des *Taches aveugles* (2012, pp. 27–29), la béance laissée par la consumation du papier carbone est celle par laquelle le dessin – un cercle noir de cendres – surgit. Dans le film *Escape Landscape* (2011, p. 38) enfin, la dislocation progressive d'une feuille de papier au contact du feu inverse le cours du temps, prenant pour point de départ sa disparition, remontant jusqu'à son état *princeps*. C'est ainsi par la défaillance ou par le manque, par une certaine *élision* de la matière que l'image se crée ou qu'elle prend corps, c'est par cette entremise que l'œuvre devient possible.

Dans une œuvre intitulée *Empreinte tacite I* (2011, p. 25), Manon Bellet représente sa propre main recouverte de poudre de graphite. Le principal outil de l'artiste prend ici l'apparence d'une sculpture figée, d'un objet à la fois précieux et inutilisable. Curieusement, cette main tant essentielle à la création ne sert plus. Elle apparaît

photographs; but also that of the engraving studio which she discovered when training at the Ecole cantonale d'art du Valais. Although her works often translate fleeting moments, many of the works of Manon Bellet are defined by loss or absence, and are screened as negatives. In the economy of means deployed, the pieces thus add nothing, or only little. They focus on an infinitely small movement, a "next to nothing," which they bring into contact with virtually impalpable forces to create a mere nuance. In the *Imagerie du hasard,* as in her very first works executed directly on the wall with an erasing pen, it is the disappearance of the original state of the substrate that gives rise to the composition. In the series of *Taches aveugles* (2012, pp. 27–29), it is through the hollowness left by the combustion of the carbon paper that the drawing – a black circle of ash – emerges. Finally, in the film *Escape Landscape* (2011, p. 38), the progressive dismemberment of a sheet of paper as it comes into contact with the flame, reverses the course of time, taking its disappearance as its starting point and reverting to its original state. It is, then, through lapse or absence, a kind of elision of the material, that the image is created or takes shape; it is through this intermediary that the work becomes possible.

In a work entitled *Empreinte tacite I* (2011, p. 25), Manon Bellet depicts her own hand covered in graphite powder.

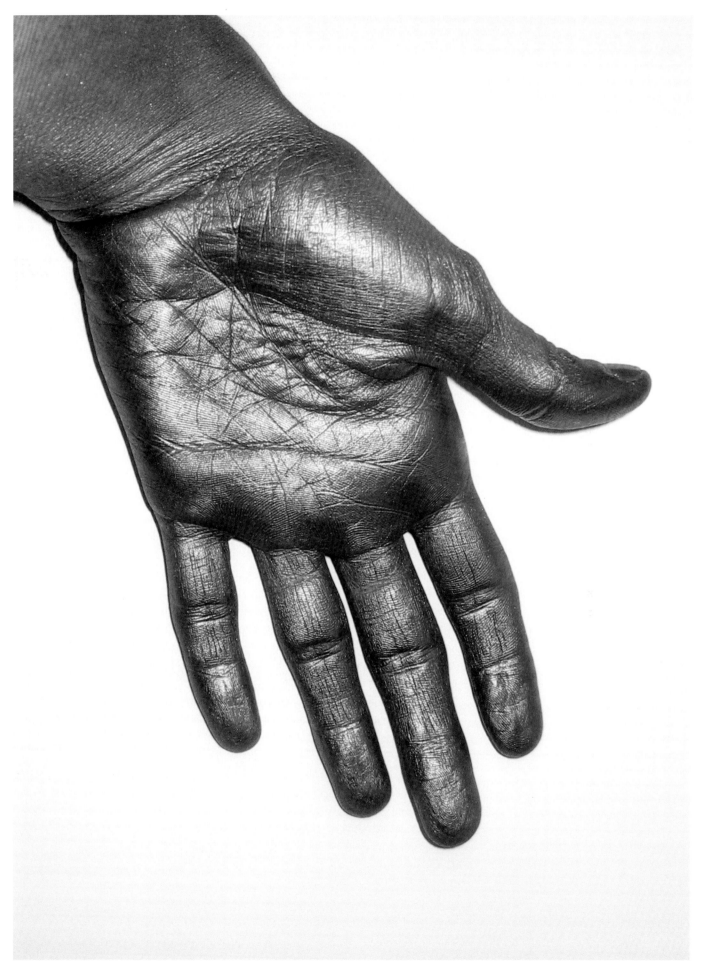

EMPREINTE TACITE I
2011

comme un bel objet, lourd et brillant. Nous sommes ici à l'opposé des matières ultrasensibles que Manon Bellet fait intervenir. Loin de leur impermanence garantie par les énergies invisibles environnantes. Dans toute l'ironie qu'elle comprend, *Empreinte tacite I* se fait la marque d'un renversement. Elle rappelle, avec humour, que le dessaisissement de la main est essentiel au travail de l'artiste. Elle peut se lire, dans ce sens, comme l'antithèse de *Vestiges* ou de *Charlotte*. Tandis que la main se fige dans sa robe cristalline, les matières inertes s'animent et se meuvent. Le travail de Manon Bellet joue de ces paradoxes. Il porte son attention sur une circulation énergétique impalpable et silencieuse immiscée dans les pans de la matière sensible pour en révéler la force. Ici, l'impermanence rencontre des forces telluriques et les matières frêles trouvent un ancrage, renvoyant ainsi à la fragilité de l'existence aussi bien qu'à son devenir.

1 Cité par Emmanuel Lequeux dans son article « Les images pénétrantes de Steve McQueen », *Le Monde,* 3 août 2013.
2 Entretien avec l'artiste dans son atelier, 4 juillet 2013. Toutes les citations suivantes en sont issues.
3 Thierry Davila, *De l'inframince. Brève histoire de l'imperceptible, de Marcel Duchamp à nos jours,* Paris : éditions du regard, Paris 2011.

1 Quoted (in French) by Emmanuel Lequeux in his article "Les images pénétrantes de Steve McQueen", *Le Monde,* 3 August 2013.
2 Interview with the artist in her studio, 4 July 2013. All the quotations that follow are from this source.
3 Thierry Davila, *De l'inframince. Brève histoire de l'imperceptible, de Marcel Duchamp à nos jours,* Paris: éditions du regard, Paris 2011.

The artist's principal instrument here appears as an immobile sculpture, an object that is at once precious and useless. Curiously, this hand that is so essential to the creative process no longer serves a purpose. It appears as a beautiful object, heavy and brilliant. We are here at the opposite end of the spectrum from the ultra-sensitive materials that Manon Bellet employs; far from their impermanence, guaranteed by the invisible energies that surround them. With all its inherent irony, *Empreinte tacite I* is an overturning of perceptions. It reminds us, with humour, that creative disengagement is essential to the work of the artist. In this sense, it can be read as the antithesis of *Vestiges* or *Charlotte.* While the hand lies motionless in its cloak of crystal, the inert materials are animated and in motion. The work of Manon Bellet plays on these paradoxes. It focuses on an impalpable, silent circulation of energy infiltrating itself among the patches of sensitive material to reveal its strength. Here, then, impermanence comes face to face with earthly forces, and the frail materials find an anchorage that reminds us of both the fragility of existence and its future.

TACHE AVEUGLE
2012

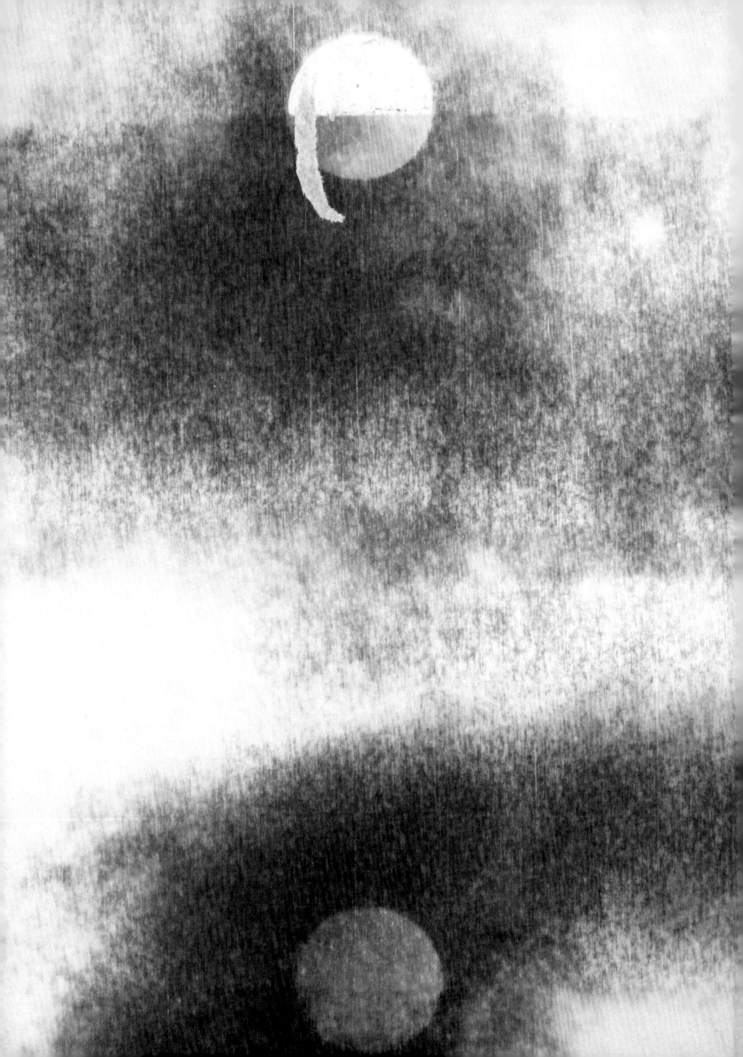

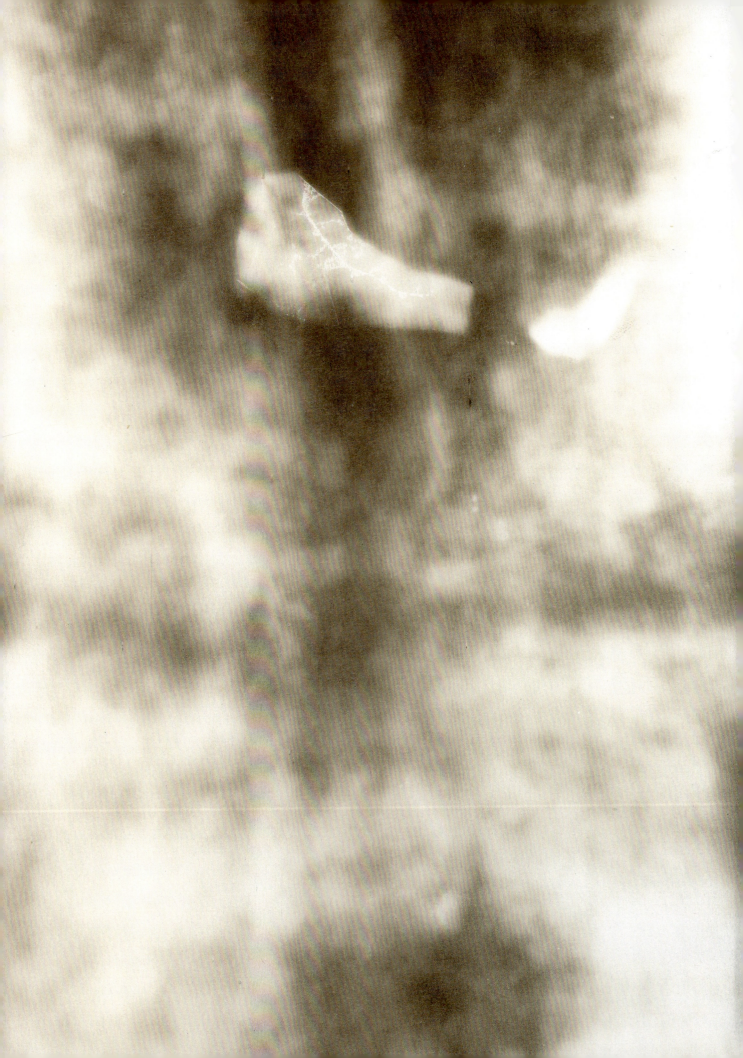

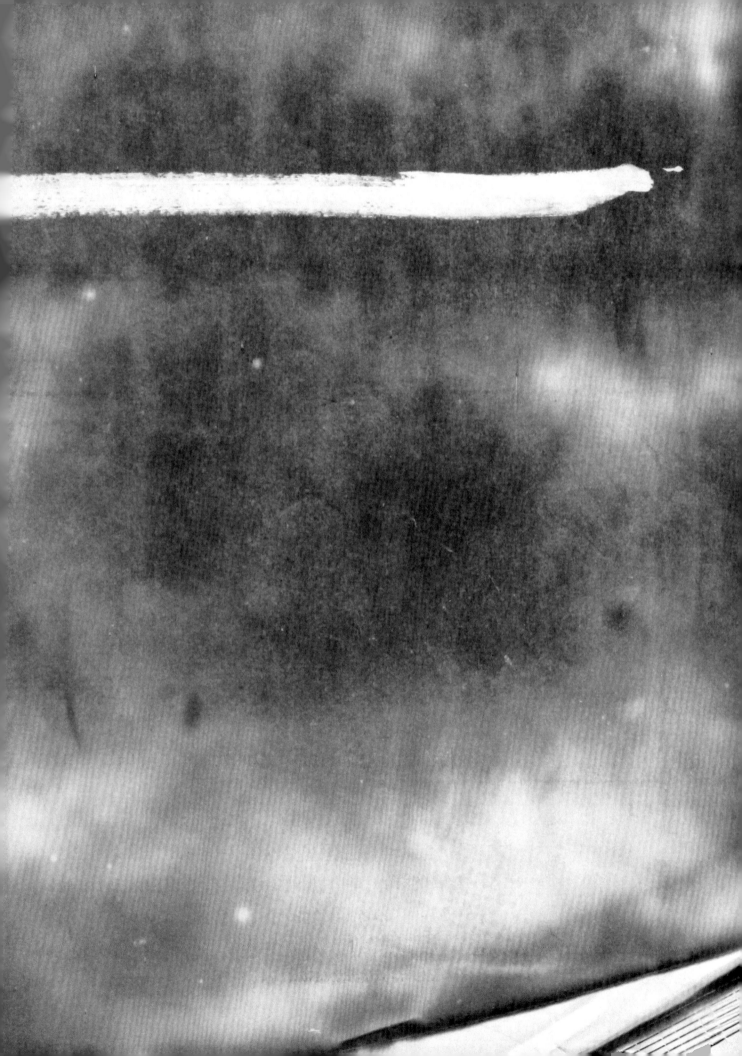

SCHATTENBILDER
Patricia Bieder

SHADOW PICTURES
Patricia Bieder

Eine dunkel verfärbte Fläche auf Manon Bellets Atelierboden erinnert als Spur an den Vorgang, der im Video *Escape Landscape* (2011, S. 38) dokumentiert ist. Die Aufnahme bietet vorerst keinen Halt, als bewege man sich beim Betrachten in einem Dazwischen, das kaum zu fassen ist. Die Arbeit ist im Fluss, transformiert sich unaufhaltsam. Der Betrachter sucht nach einer Verortung: Handelt es sich um eine Ansammlung von Wasser am Boden, in der sich das Vorbeiziehen der Wolken spiegelt? Oder ist es eine Aufnahme einer Landschaft aus der Vogelperspektive, wofür der Titel sprechen könnte? Die Langsamkeit des Videos lässt verschiedene Assoziationen zu, bis dann Unsicherheit und Zweifel in Gewissheit, Fiktion in Realität übergehen. Es sind die sich langsam verändernden dunklen und hellen Formen, ein eigentliches Spiel von Positiv- und Negativformen, welche die Aufmerksamkeit auf sich ziehen, wobei die weissen Flächen immer mehr an Oberhand gewinnen und dem Auge Halt geben. Fast surreal anmutend, scheinen sich die Flammen zurück zu ziehen, ohne Spuren zu hinterlassen. Schliesslich sind es die weissen Negativformen, die erkennen lassen, dass es sich um eine mehrere Minuten dauernde Aufnahme im Rücklauf handelt, in der Feuer ein Blatt Papier zersetzt.

In *Escape Landscape* eröffnet sich auf dem Papier eine faszinierende Welt, deren imaginäre Räume sich immer wieder verändern, bis die weisse Fläche des Blattes die Arbeit

A dark patch on the floor of Manon Bellet's studio recalls the process that is documented in the video *Escape Landscape* (2011, p. 38). The image in the video makes it hard to find one's bearings, it is as though one were in a barely comprehensible midway zone. The work is in flux, constantly changing. The viewer seeks some point of orientation: is this a patch of water on the ground, with reflections of the clouds passing overhead? Or is it a bird's-eye view of a landscape, which might tally with the title? The slowness of the video provides scope for various associations, until uncertainty and doubt become conviction and fiction becomes reality. The viewer's attention is caught by slowly changing dark and light forms, an ongoing interplay of positive and negative, with the areas of white increasingly gaining the upper hand and making sense to the eye. In an almost surreal manner, the flames seem to recede without leaving a trace. Ultimately it is the white negative forms that reveal that this scene lasting several minutes is in fact a video, played backwards, of fire destroying a piece of paper.

In *Escape Landscape* a fascinating world appears, constantly mutating until the white surface of the sheet of paper situates the work in reality. By showing the process of burning, the annihilation of the paper, as a rewind, the artist progressively reveals its appearance as

in der Realität situiert. Indem die Künstlerin den Prozess des Verbrennens, des Auslöschens im *rewind* zeigt, wird in der Zerstörung des Papiers dessen Erscheinen als weisse Fläche sichtbar. Die Auseinandersetzung mit dem Phänomen des Erscheinens und Verschwindens, in dem das Auslöschen nicht zu einem Nichts, sondern zu neuer produktiver Formgebung führt, beschäftigt die Künstlerin in ihrer künstlerischen Arbeit. Bereits in ihren frühen grossen Wandzeichnungen erprobte Manon Bellet mit Tinte und Tintenlöscher den Übergang zwischen Leere und Fülle. Diese künstlerische Haltung legt den Fokus nicht auf das fertige Werk und dessen Dauerhaftigkeit, sondern interessiert sich für die Transformation und das Ephemere. Es ist eine Haltung, die mit dem für Manon Bellet wichtigen Zitat des Fluxus-Künstlers George Brecht (1926–2008) beschrieben werden kann: „You don't have to worry about whether you are doing research or not. You only have to know that what you do has an unforeseen outcome."[1] Der von den Vertretern der Fluxus-Bewegung in den 1960er Jahren vertretene experimentelle Ansatz, nach dem die Verwischung der Medien sowie die Betonung der schöpferischen Idee im Gegensatz zum abgeschlossenen Kunstwerk steht, findet sich auch im Werk von Manon Bellet. Das lateinische Wort ‚Fluxus' bedeutet ‚fliessend, veränderlich', und so kann auch ihre Kunst beschrieben werden. Manon Bellets Kunst ist im Fluss. Ihre Wachheit und Offenheit gegenüber der Gegenwart

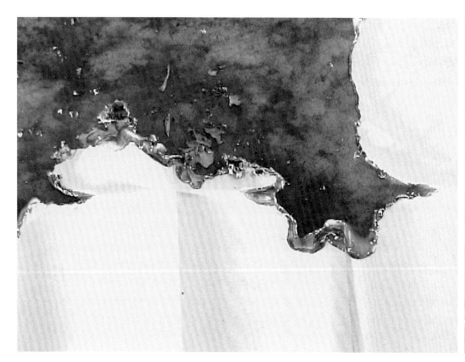

machen die Arbeiten fliessend und veränderlich wie die Ideen und Materialien, aus denen sie bestehen.

Manon Bellet arbeitet vorwiegend mit Papier. Selbst in ihren Videoarbeiten wird es oft zum medialen Mittelpunkt. Sie bedient sich dabei vor allem dünner, delikater, häufig auch wärme- und lichtempfindlicher Papiere, wie Thermo-, Seiden- oder Kohlepapier, deren spezifische Eigenschaften – Fragilität und Verletzlichkeit – sie besonders interessieren. Sie rückt damit auch die materielle Beschaffenheit der Papiere in den Blick. Auch Papierreste, wie zum Beispiel die mit einem Klebepunkt versehenen Enden von Thermopapierrollen werden aufgrund der strukturellen Unregelmässigkeiten für die Künstlerin reizvoll. Obwohl sie sich vorwiegend mit Papier beschäftigt, benutzt sie es kaum für Zeichnungen im herkömmlichen Sinn. Die direkte künstlerische Geste bleibt selten, die Spur ihrer Hand ist fast immer verborgen. Stattdessen sind es Spuren thermischer oder magnetischer Verfahren, die Aufnahmen von Licht und Schatten oder die Resultate von Verbrennungsvorgängen, die ihre Kunst prägen und auf diese Weise Zeichen entstehen lassen, die neu gelesen werden können. Anstelle von Bleistift, Kohle oder Tusche finden sich auf ihrer Arbeitsfläche im Atelier etwa kleine Metallteile, deren Enden Manon Bellet mit Feuer erhitzt und zum Beispiel in den „croquis de chaleur" (2012–2013, S. 64–71) über das Thermopapier bewegt, bis die Wärme entschwindet. In der Reaktion mit der

a white plane. This confrontation with the phenomenon of appearance and disappearance, with annihilation leading not to nothingness but to productive form-giving, is a longstanding theme in Manon Bellet's artistic work. In her early, large-format wall drawings she already used ink and ink remover to explore the transition between a blank space and abundance. This artistic approach focuses not on the finished work and its longevity but concentrates instead on transformation and the ephemeral. It is a stance that could be described in the words of the Fluxus artist George Brecht (1926–2008), whose thinking is important to Manon Bellet: "You don't have to worry about whether you are doing research or not. You only have to know that what you do has an unforeseen outcome."[1] The experimental approach taken by exponents of Fluxus in the 1960s, who valued the mingling of different media and the emphasis on the creative idea as opposed to the finished work of art, lives on in the work of Manon Bellet. The Latin word *fluxus* means "fluid" or "changeable," both of which can also be applied to her art. Manon Bellet's art is in flux. Her alertness and openness to the present give her works the same fluidity and changeability as the ideas and materials from which they are made. Manon Bellet predominantly works with paper. Even in her video works the medium of paper often takes center

Hitze tauchen auf dem wärmeempfindlichen Papier dunkle Spuren auf, Linien und Flächen, die an feine Tuschezeichnungen erinnern. Die „croquis de chaleur" verdeutlichen die Haltung der Künstlerin: Sie regt Prozesse an, die zu Transformationen der Materialien führen. Dabei richtet sie den Blick auf Veränderungen von Strukturen und Spuren, beobachtet und macht den Moment des Übergangs, der Hervorbringung, sichtbar. Ihr Atelier wird zu einem Labor, einem Ort der Materialforschung, der Form- und Dingerfindung. Auch ihre Notizhefte erzählen von Beobachtungen, Ideen und Gedanken oder kleinen Experimenten, die zu künftigen Arbeiten Anstoss geben könnten.

Der Forschergeist, der sie antreibt, kann mit dem Serendipitäts-Prinzip umschrieben werden. Der Begriff ‚Serendipität' meint, etwas zu finden, was nicht ursprüngliches Ziel war und geht auf das persische Märchen der drei Prinzen von Serendip zurück, die die Begabung hatten, aus zufälligen und unerwarteten Entdeckungen Schlüsse zu ziehen. Oft lässt sich Manon Bellet intuitiv von Prozessen leiten, lässt sich gerne überraschen, arbeitet mit den Zeichen, die der Zufall beschert. *Sérendipité* (2010, S. 41) heisst denn auch eine von Manon Bellets Werkgruppen, in denen sie die Spuren interessieren, die sich durch das Ansengen des gefalteten weissen Papiers ergeben haben. Das Resultat überrascht auch die Künstlerin, da sie nicht genau weiss, wie die angesengten Ränder auf der

stage. Above all she uses fine, delicate paper, which is frequently also sensitive to warmth and light, as in the case of thermal, silk, and charcoal paper, whose salient features – fragility and vulnerability – are of particular interest to her. She thus draws attention to the material nature of these different types of paper. Paper remnants, such as the ends of rolls of thermal paper with a spot of glue on them, also have a special appeal for Manon Bellet because of their structural irregularities. Although she mainly works with paper, she rarely uses it for drawings in the traditional sense. She seldom goes in for direct, artistic gestures; any indications of the presence of her hand are almost always hidden. Instead her work is pervaded by traces of thermal or magnetic processes, shots of light and shadows, or the results of fiery processes, creating signs that can be read in new ways. Rather than pencil, charcoal, or ink, lying on Manon Bellet's work desk in her studio there are little pieces of metal, which can be heated at one end and, in the "croquis de chaleur" (2012–2013, pp. 64–71) for instance, passed across thermal paper until all the heat has escaped. As the heat-sensitive paper reacts dark marks appear, lines and planes that recall delicate ink drawings. Manon Bellet's "croquis de chaleur" exemplify her approach, for in these she instigates processes that lead to the transformation of a

aufgefalteten Unterlage wirken. Die Zerstörung wird zum Akt der Neuschöpfung. Der langsame Zerfall der Arbeit, der sich in Form von kleinsten Teilchen, die sich im Bildrahmen sammeln, offenbart, weckt das Interesse der Künstlerin.

Für ihre erste museale Einzelausstellung und die Publikation hat Manon Bellet den Titel *L'onde d'une ombre* gewählt. Welle und Schatten erinnern in ihrer Immaterialität und Flüchtigkeit an das Unfassbare und Vergängliche. Wie der Schatten, der sich als flüchtiges Abbild zeigt und einer Welle gleich sich über die Oberfläche bewegt, begreifen die Werke von Manon Bellet als ‚Schattenbilder' das Fliessen der Zeit, machen die Spur sichtbar, in der sich „Präsenz und Absenz, Sichtbarkeit und Unsichtbarkeit, Gegenwart und Vergangenheit"[2] kreuzen. Schattenbilder sind sie, weil sich in ihnen die Bewegung von immateriellen und flexiblen Elementen wie Feuer, Licht oder Hitze sichtbar niederschlägt. Der Augenblick, der sich einem Schatten gleich ins Trägermaterial einzuschreiben scheint, ist etwa in der Werkgruppe *Imagerie du hasard* (2011–2012, S. 30–35) thematisiert: Es handelt sich um Arbeiten, in denen das Licht und die Wärme als Abdruck neue Bildwelten schaffen. Thermopapier das für einige Minuten auf eine von der Sonne erhitzte Metallplatte gelegt wird, verfärbt sich an manchen Stellen dunkel. Manon Bellet lässt hierfür den Zufall spielen, gleichwohl ist das entstandene Bild eine von ihr kontrollierte Komposition. Mit den dunklen Verfärbungen, den Unschärfen

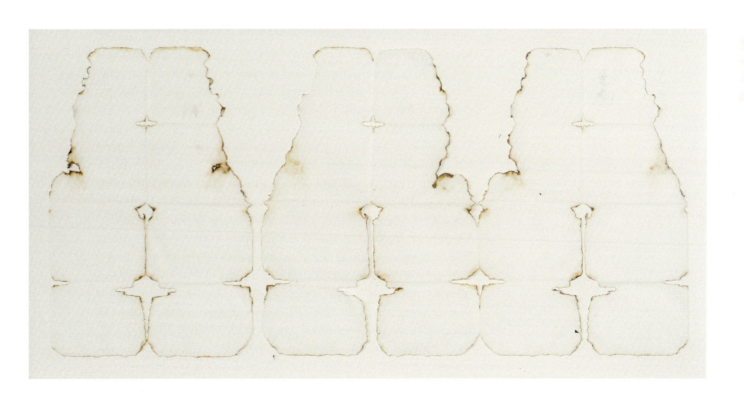

SÉRENDIPITÉ
2010

 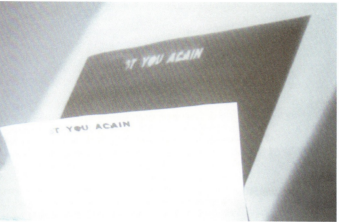

und den fliessenden Übergängen, die durch die Spuren von Licht und Wärme entstanden sind sowie die häufig auftretenden Kreisscheiben, die ursprünglich die Enden der Thermopapierrollen markierten, evozieren die Arbeiten Mondnächte und Nebelszenen von malerischer, ja romantischer Bildwirkung und lassen stilistisch an frühe fotografische Himmelsstudien denken.

Oder aber der Schatten wird zum Motiv und evoziert ein wirkliches Schattenbild, ja Schattenspiel, wie im Video *I Lost You Again* (2009, S. 42–43), das vom Schatten und dem sich verändernden Augenblick ausgeht. In dieser Arbeit setzt sich die

given material. Her interest is in changes in structures and the traces left by these processes; she observes and renders visible the moment of transition, of production. Her studio is more like a laboratory, where materials are researched, where forms and things may be invented. Her notebooks also tell of observations, ideas, and thoughts, or small experiments that could provide the stimulus for future works.

The spirit of enquiry that motivates Manon Bellet could be likened to a belief in serendipity, a term that dates back to the tale of the *Three Princes of Serendip* who had a natural gift for making useful discoveries quite by accident. Manon Bellet often intuitively allows herself to be guided by processes she has set in motion; she enjoys being taken by surprise. *Sérendipité* (2010, p. 41) is the title of a group of works in which the focus was on the scorch marks on a piece of folded, white paper. The result was a surprise even to the artist, for she could not know exactly how the scorched edges would affect the folded paper lower down. This process of destruction becomes an act of new creation. The gradual disintegration of the work, which is seen in the form of tiny particles collecting in the picture frame, is also of interest to the artist.

The title Manon Bellet chose for her first museum exhibition and the publication was *L'onde d'une ombre* [The

Wave of a Shadow]. In their immateriality and evanescence wave and shadow call to mind things ungraspable and transient. Like the shadow that appears as a fleeting likeness and moves wave-like on a surface, Manon Bellet's "shadow pictures" capture the flow of time, giving visual form to the moment when "presence and absence, visibility and invisibility, the present and the past"[2] intersect. They are shadow pictures because they contain the evidence of the movement of immaterial, fluctuating elements such as fire, light, and heat. The moment that seems to inscribe itself into the supporting material like a shadow is seen for instance in the series of works *Imagerie du hasard* (2011–2012, pp. 30–35): these are works where the imprints of light and warmth generate new pictorial worlds. If thermal paper is laid for a few minutes on a metal plate heated by the sun, it will darken in places. Manon Bellet invites chance to play its part in this, although the resulting image is still undoubtedly a

I LOST YOU AGAIN
2009

Künstlerin mit dem Lauf der Zeit auseinander, der im Wechselspiel von Erscheinen und Verschwinden nachvollziehbar wird. Auf einem weissen Blatt Papier, das gefaltet auf dem Tisch steht, sind die Worte des Satzes ‚I lost you again' ausgeschnitten. Die Buchstaben werden zur Schablone, durch die das Sonnenlicht fällt und im Schlagschatten des Papiers als weisses Sprachbild aufleuchtet. Während einer Stunde filmte Manon Bellet den sich verändernden Lichteinfall. Je nach Sonneneinstrahlung zeichnen sich die Worte als Schattenbild auf der Tischfläche unterschiedlich ab. Sobald die Buchstaben auf der Tischplatte erscheinen, verlieren sie sich auf dem Papier. Als Betrachter folgen wir dem Kommen und Gehen des projizierten Satzes, lesen die Wörter, um im Verschwinden des Satzes das Verlieren zu erfahren. Auf dem Blatt wie in seiner ‚Projektion' bleibt der Satz ungreifbar und verweist damit bereits auf seinen Inhalt. Er macht aber auch deutlich, dass die Zeit eine unfassbare Grösse ist, die mit jedem Augenblick verrinnt. Die durch das Sonnenlicht abgebildete Aussage erscheint so flüchtig wie der Schatten. Seine stete Veränderung wiederum erinnert an den kontinuierlichen Verlust.

Den ausgesprochen langsamen, gar meditativ anmutenden Videoarbeiten von Manon Bellet liegt eine nicht-narrative Struktur zugrunde, worauf auch die leeren Seiten in der Videoarbeit *Vestiges* (2010, S. 20–22) hinweisen können. Anstelle des Erzählerischen werden, wie bereits bei *Escape Landscape*,

composition of her own making. With their dark coloration, blurred edges, and fluid transitions – resulting from the influence of light and warmth – and the many circular discs that originally marked the ends of the rolls of thermal paper, these works seem to evoke moonlit nights and misty scenes with a picturesque, even Romantic air, all of which call to mind early photographic studies of the sky. Elsewhere the shadow becomes the motif and evokes a real shadow image, even a shadow play, as in the video *I Lost You Again* (2009, pp. 42–43), which toys with a shadow and a changing moment. In this work the artist engages with the passage of time, which makes itself felt in the interplay of appearance and disappearance. The words of the sentence "I lost you again," in capital letters, are cut out of a sheet of folded white paper placed on a table. The sunlight passes through the cut-out letters and appears as white writing in the shadow cast by the paper. For an hour Manon Bellet filmed the paper in the changing light. The angle and strength of the sun affects the appearance of the words in the shadow on the table. As soon as the words appear on the table top, they disappear from the paper. As viewers we observe the coming and going of the projected sentence, we read the words, and as the sentence vanishes we experience a sense of loss. The sentence, both as cut-out words and in its

Räume geöffnet, die mit Assoziationen und Geschichten der Betrachtenden gefüllt werden können. Während die Buchstaben auf den lichten Seiten bereits verschwunden scheinen, ist das Buch mit seinen leeren, vergilbt wirkenden Seiten als Relikt übrig geblieben, wie es der Werktitel suggeriert. Ein sanfter Luftzug bewegt die Seiten langsam und scheint gleichsam im Buch zu blättern. Dabei nehmen die feinen, transparenten Seiten immer wieder neue Formen an und erinnern an Kompositionen der konstruktivistischen Kunst. Mit jeder neuen Überlagerung ändert sich die Lichtwirkung. Neben dieser zufälligen und wortlosen Form-Geschichte lädt das Buch zu eigenen Projektionen ein. Die Videoarbeit mahnt mit ihren verblassten Seiten nicht nur an die Vergänglichkeit, das sich aufblätternde Buch betont zugleich die Schnittstelle zwischen Vergangenheit und Zukunft, zwischen Erinnerung und Wunsch. In diesem Augenblick des Innehaltens und der Reflexion spiegelt sich die Fragilität von Dingen, ja des Lebens schlechthin. Das Vor- oder Zurückblättern in der eigenen Biografie bietet nur unsichere Einsichten an, sind die aufgeschlagenen Seiten und Ansichten doch dem Zufall des Windes überlassen.

Überlagerungen, wie sie in den filmischen Arbeiten *I Lost You Again* oder *Vestiges* vorkommen, zeigen sich auch in verschiedenen Werkgruppen auf Papier, wie der Cyanotypie-Serie *Sous sur face* (2012–2013, S. 47–52, 55). Der Kunststoff, den Manon Bellet hier in Form von durchsichtigen

"projection," is ungraspable and as such already points to its own meaning. However, it also makes clear that time is an unfathomable component that is constantly trickling away. The statement formed by sunlight is as fleeting as the shadow. And its ongoing mutations are a reminder of that continuous loss.

These strikingly slow, maybe even meditative video works by Manon Bellet are non-narrative in their structure, like the empty pages of the video work *Vestiges* (2010, pp. 20–22). As earlier on, in *Escape Landscape,* instead of launching into narration the video opens up spaces that can be filled with the viewer's own associations and stories. Whereas it appears that the letters on the pale pages have already vanished, the book, as the title of the work suggests, is left behind as a relic, with empty, faded pages. A gentle current of air slowly moves the pages, as though it were leafing through the book. Yet these same fine, transparent pages are constantly taking on new forms in a manner that is reminiscent of compositions by Constructivist artists. With every new layering the light effects change. Beside revealing this fortuitous, wordless form-story the book also invites viewers to make their own projections. The faded pages of this video work are not only a reminder of transience, as they turn the book also reminds us of the interface between the past and the

Plastiktüten verwendet, ist für sie aufgrund seiner minderen Qualität, seiner Feinheit und Transparenz reizvoll. Die Cyanotypie ist ein Edeldruckverfahren, das in den 40er Jahren des 19. Jahrhunderts entwickelt wurde. Dabei wird ein Papier in eine lichtempfindliche Lösung eingetaucht und im Dunkeln getrocknet. Anschliessend wird auf die lichtempfindliche Beschichtung eine Vorlage gelegt. Die Belichtung mit Sonnenlicht hinterlässt Abdrücke auf dem Blatt, die durch abschliessende chemische Entwicklungsvorgänge als helle Schatten auf dem mit ‚Berliner Blau' gefärbten Papier sichtbar werden. Die weichen Abbilder in *Sous sur face* haben sich von der üblichen Wahrnehmung von Plastiktüten entfernt und erinnern in ihrer Durchsichtigkeit und Mehrschichtigkeit eher an organische Formen. Es scheint, als sei es durch die Berührung des Lichts zu einer Verlebendigung des künstlichen Plastiks gekommen, der sich nun, gallertartigen Organismen gleich, schwerelos bewegt. Damit gelingt es Manon Bellet, den synthetischen Stoff subtil als plastisches Material zu zeigen und dessen Oberflächenstruktur hervorzuheben. Das Plastik wird verlebendigt, wobei es in *Sous sur face* „weniger Gegenstand als Spur einer Bewegung"[3] verkörpert. *Sous sur face* zeigt exemplarisch, wie sorgfältig und reflektiert Manon Bellet bei der Wahl der Werktitel vorgeht. Mit der paradoxen Umdrehung von Ober- und Unterfläche, die in *Sous sur face* anklingt, verweist der Titel auf ein Dazwischen, das zeitlich, räumlich oder

future, between memories and desires. This moment of contemplation, when time seems to stand still, reflects the fragility of things, of life itself. Leafing forward and back in one's own life story can only yield uncertain insights, for the pages and sights that come into view are a random selection generated by the wind.
Layers, as in the video works *I lost you again* and *Vestiges*, are also seen in various groups of works on paper, such as the series of cyanotypes, *Sous sur face* (2012–2013, pp. 47–52, 55). The synthetic material that Manon Bellet uses here, namely transparent plastic bags, appeals to her because of its inferior quality, thinness, and transparence. The cyanotype is a time-honored printing process that was developed in the 1840s. Paper is coated in a light-sensitive solution and dried in darkness. Following this the object to be reproduced is laid on the paper. Exposure to sunlight creates an imprint on the paper, which, following chemical developing processes, appears as a pale shadow on the paper colored with Prussian blue. The soft images in *Sous sur face* have little to do with the usual perception of plastic bags and, in their translucence and multiple layers, seem closer to organic forms. It is as though the contact with light has breathed life into the plastic bags, which now float weightlessly, like gelatinous organisms. Manon Bellet thus presents the synthetic

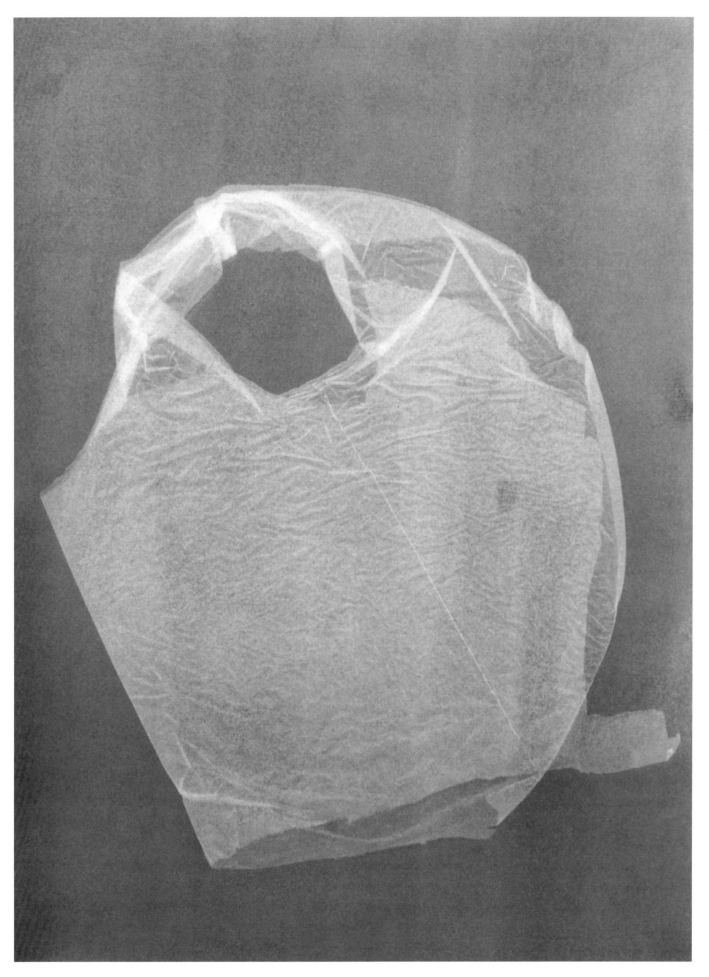

SOUS SUR FACE
2013

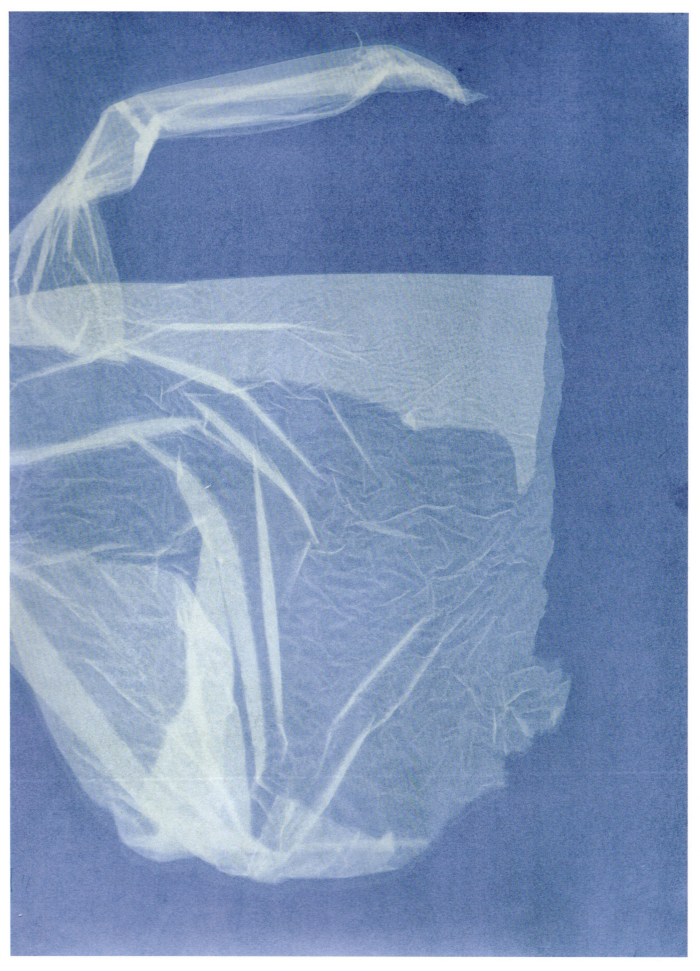

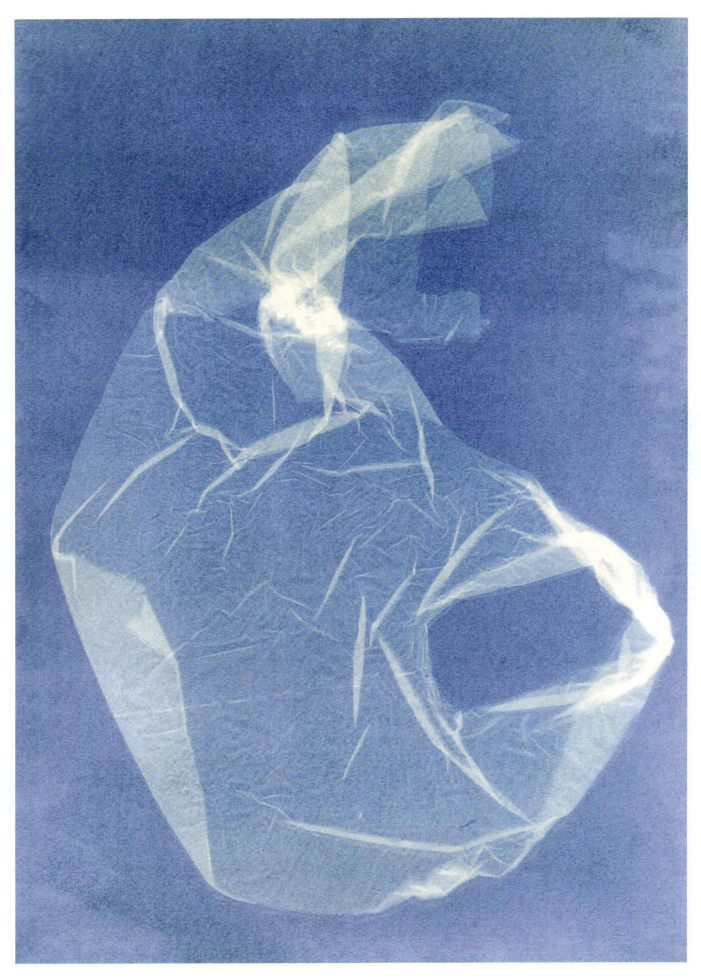

SOUS SUR FACE
2013

SOUS SUR FACE
2012

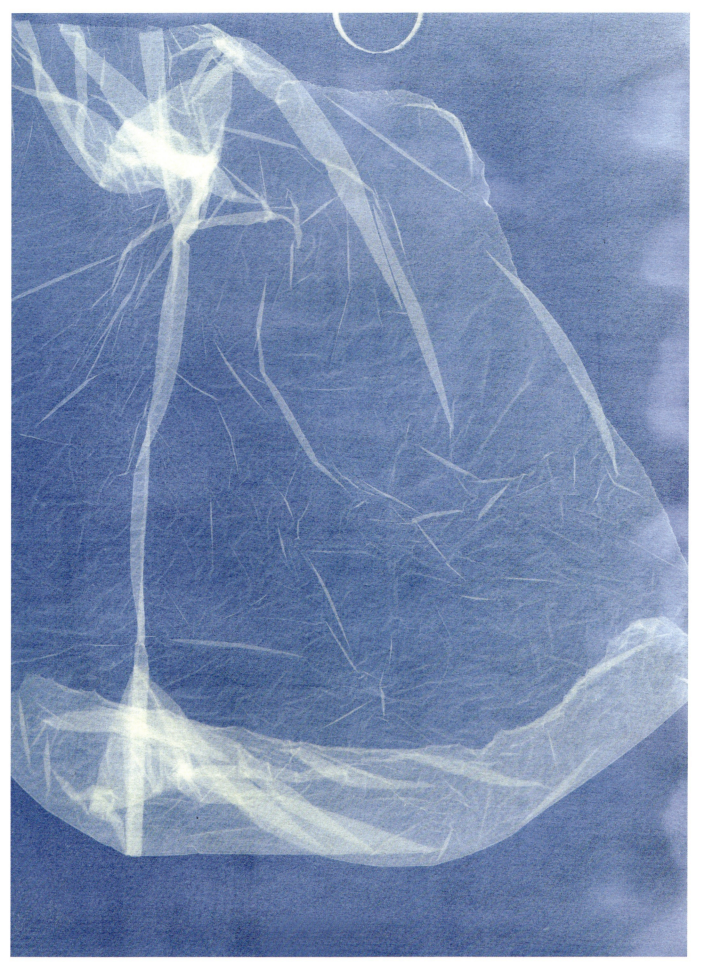

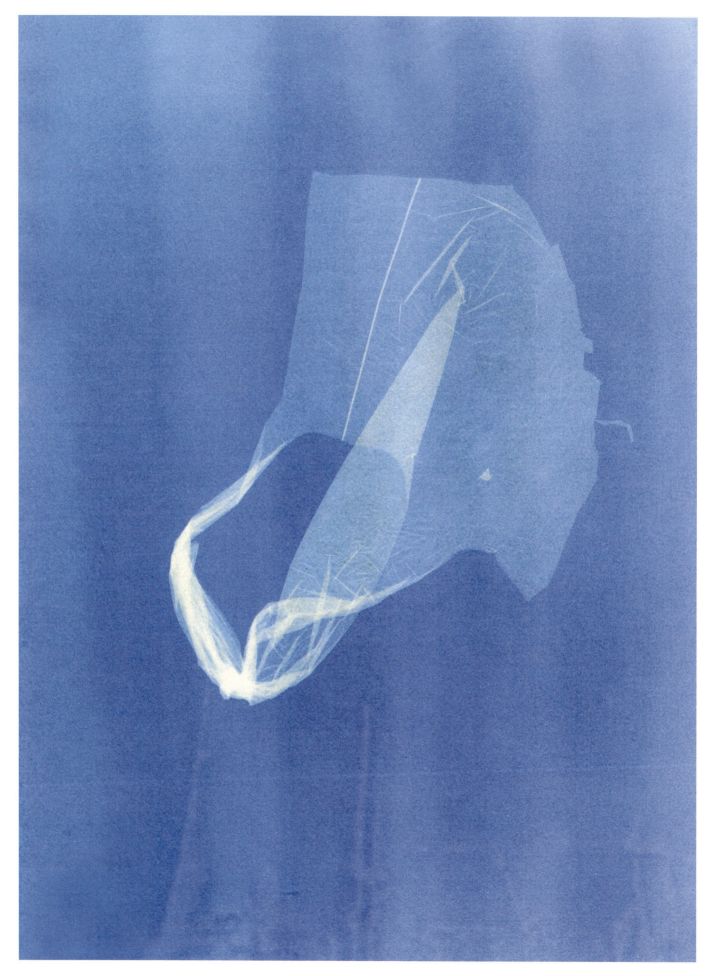

SOUS SUR FACE
2013

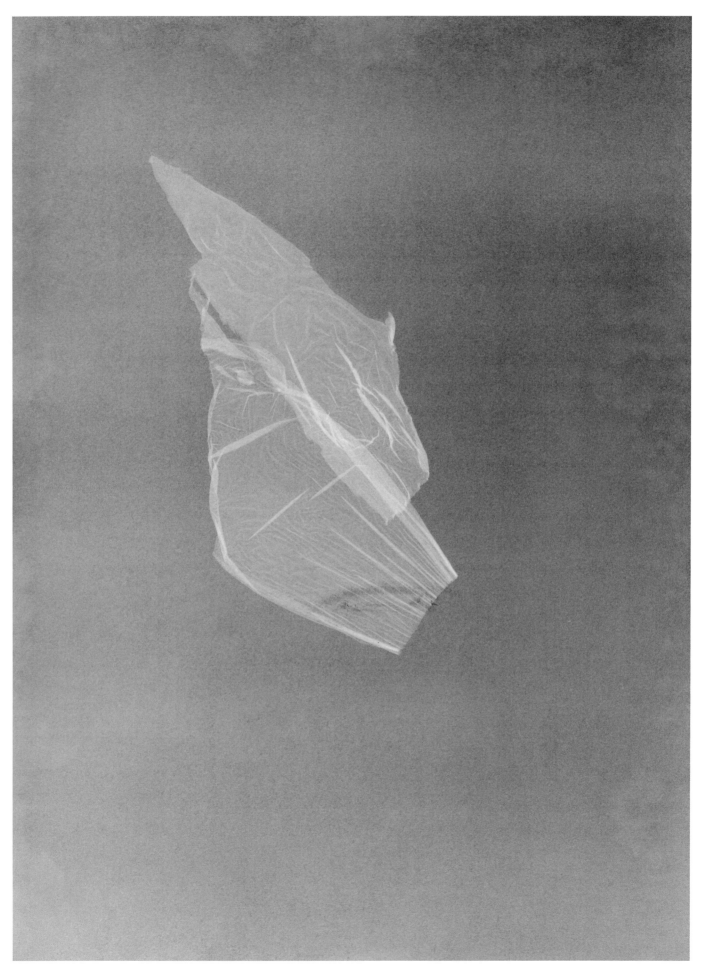

mental verstanden werden kann. Die Titel, oft neue Wortbildungen, Wortspielereien oder Andeutungen ermöglichen eine spezifische Interpretation der Arbeiten. Aber selbst solche Fingerzeige sind nur Ausgangspunkt eines Denkprozesses, den die Werke in ihrer Komplexität einfordern.

Eine ähnliche mediale und gedankliche Überlagerung von vorgestellten und konkreten Realitäten zeigt sich in der fotografischen Serie *Le rideau dans le tableau* (2009, S. 107/109) an. In diesen drei Arbeiten führt der komplexe Arbeitsprozess, in dem verschiedene Medien und Techniken kombiniert werden, zu einem rätselhaften Entstehen und Verschwinden von Formen und Figuren auf dem Papier. Dafür fotografierte Manon Bellet die Projektion eines Dias, das sie zuvor bemalt hatte. Der Schatten der Künstlerin fügt hier eine weitere Ebene, eine weitere Spur hinzu. Zuletzt wurden diese Fotografien auf Aquarellpapier gedruckt, was zu einer malerischen Atmosphäre der Arbeiten führt. Auf subtile Art wird mit dem Schatten der Künstlerin die Arbeit zu einem Selbstporträt, das sich aber immer in einem Spannungsfeld zwischen Auflösung und Erscheinung bewegt. Eigentliche Schattenbilder, wie in *Le rideau dans le tableau*, begegnen uns auch in den Serien *Sun Two I* & *Sun Two II* (2009, S. 56) und *Idole I* & *Idole II* (2009, S. 56). Als Vorlage liegen eigene und fremde Bilder zugrunde, die Manon Bellet mittels Frottage auf das Papier überträgt. Es entstehen Schattenbilder: Durch die Technik des Indirekten

material as a malleable substance, drawing particular attention to its surface structure. The plastic comes to life, although in *Sous sur face* "it is less a thing than the trace of a movement."[3] *Sous sur face* perfectly demonstrates how carefully and thoughtfully Manon Bellet chooses the titles of her works. The paradoxical reversal of surfaces above and below that is hinted at in the title *Sous sur face* suggests a midway realm either conceptually or in terms of time and space. Bellet's titles, often containing neologisms, word plays, or allusions, allow the viewer to embark on a specific interpretation of her works. But even these pointers are only the starting point for the lengthy thought processes that these complex works demand.

A similar layering, both conceptually and in terms of artistic media, is seen in the three-part photographic series *Le rideau dans le tableau* (2009, pp. 107/109). In these works on paper the complex artistic process, combining different media and techniques, leads to a bewildering manifestation and evaporation of forms and figures. In the creation of this work, Manon Bellet photographed a projection of a slide that she had previously painted. The shadow of the artist adds another level, another trace. These photographs were then printed on watercolor paper, which gives the images a painterly atmosphere. The presence of the artist's own shadow subtly turns

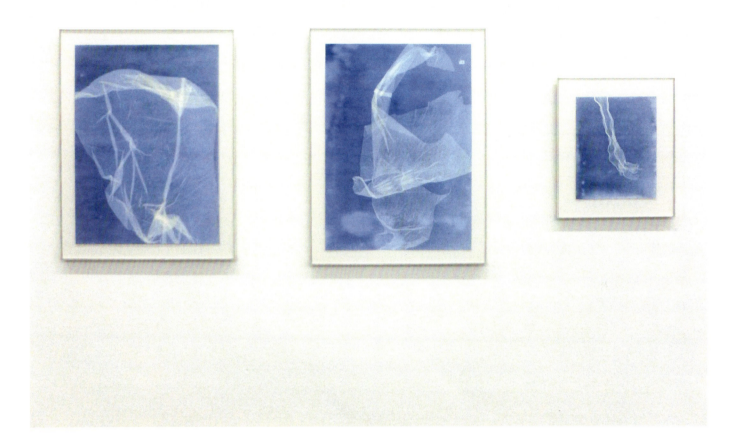

the work into a self-portrait, although it is always poised somewhere between dissolution and materialization. Actual shadow images, as in *Le rideau dans le tableau,* also appear in the series *Sun Two I* & *Sun Two II* (2009, p. 56) and *Idole I* & *Idole II* (2009, p. 56). The basis for these works are pictures by Manon Bellet herself and by others, which she transferred onto the paper using *frottage.* The resulting images could be described as shadow pictures: this indirect technique causes the original motifs to lose their sharpness. They become diffuse likenesses that spur the viewer's imagination into activity. The random aspect of frottages, which were particularly favored by the Surrealists, is intended to stir the imagination. Any interpretations of the ensuing images are affected by chance, personal preferences, and the viewer's sense of creative freedom. Manon Bellet's frottages are reminiscent of the patches on a wall that Leonardo da Vinci saw as a source of individual, artistic inspiration. The artist's

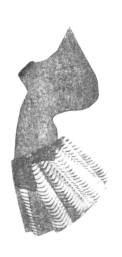 

▲ IDOLE I & IDOLE II
2009

SUN TWO I & SUN TWO II
2009

verliert das ursprüngliche Motiv an Schärfe und wird zu einem diffusen Abbild, das die Imagination anregt. Die zufälligen Erscheinungen der Frottagen, die besonders von den Surrealisten eingesetzt wurden, sollen das Imaginieren anregen. Die Interpretationen des Gesehenen haben mit Zufall, persönlicher Neigung und der kreativen Freiheit des Betrachters zu tun. Manon Bellets Frottagen erinnern an Leonardo Da Vincis Wandflecken, die zu immer neuen individuellen Bildfindungen führen. Der direkte Eingriff führt den Prozess der ‚Einbildung' vor: So verleihen die kurzen Bleistiftstriche, mit denen die Künstlerin vereinzelt in die sonst von der Technik des Indirekten geprägten Arbeiten eingreift, dem Druck Tiefe. Sie mögen die Idee von fliegenden Vögeln vorbringen, welche die geometrischen Formen als Berglandschaften sehen lassen. In *Idole I* & *Idole II* entsteht eine Abfolge von Formen, die wie Figuren und in tänzerischen Bewegungen das Papier strukturieren und den Eindruck einer vergangenen Zeit erwecken. Was wir sehen hängt mit persönlicher Erinnerung und Einbildungskraft zusammen. Insofern sind die beiden Serien als Schattenbilder auch ein Versuch, den kreativen Prozess der Imagination zu zeigen.

Immer wieder beschäftigt sich Manon Bellet mit dem archaischen Element des Feuers. Sie macht damit den Moment eines Übergangs oder Wandels erkennbar. Dabei wird insbesondere im Umgang mit Feuer die Balance zwischen

direct intervention demonstrates the imaginative flights the viewer might pursue in his or her mind: the short, isolated pencil marks that the artist makes in these works that are otherwise formed solely by chance, add depth to the print. These marks may call to mind birds in flight, with the geometrical forms taking on the aspect of mountainous landscapes. In *Idole I* & *Idole II* a sequence of forms – like figures performing dancelike movements – structure the paper and create the impression of a long-lost era. What we see in these images depends on our own personal memories and powers of imagination. In that sense both these series of shadow pictures are also an attempt to demonstrate the creative process of the imagination.

Manon Bellet has repeatedly engaged with the archaic element of fire. In so doing she clearly marks the moment of transition or change. At the same time, the way she handles fire particularly highlights the balance she achieves between creation and destruction, which she is constantly seeking out and experimenting with. However, in most of her works the flames of any fire do not come into view, as they do so often in the work of Roman Signer (*1938), where they may be seen as an "expression of utmost presentness."[4] On the contrary, in Manon Bellet's hands the traces of fire bear witness to a past

BRÈVE BRAISE
2011

Gestaltungs- und Zerstörungskraft sichtbar, die die Künstlerin immer wieder neu sucht und erforscht. In den meisten Arbeiten aber sind nicht die Flammen selbst zu sehen, wie sie beispielsweise bei Roman Signer (*1938) häufig auftreten und dort zum „Ausdruck höchster Gegenwärtigkeit"[4] werden. Vielmehr bezeugen die Spuren bei Manon Bellet ein vergangenes Brennen und werden damit zu „gedächtnisfähigen Materialien", denen Erinnerungen eingeschrieben sind. Indem die Arbeiten ein vergangenes Brennen suggerieren, „werden sie zu einem Speicher",[5] wie Monika Wagner in ihrer Untersuchung zum *Material in der Moderne* festhält. In *Burning Line* (2010–2011, S. 62–63) etwa sind durch Ansengen von Seidenpapier verkohlte Ränder entstanden. Je nach Eingriff und Hitze, die vom kontrollierten Umgang mit dem Feuer zeugen, bilden die Spuren unterschiedlich grosse Positiv-Negativ Formen, die sich zu ‚gezeichneten' Silhouetten schliessen. Die verkohlten Papierränder erinnern an feine Kohlezeichnungen, auch wenn sie nicht durch die Hand der Künstlerin, sondern als Spur des Feuers entstanden sind: Im wahrsten Sinne des Wortes handelt es sich um Kohlezeichnungen. Sie lassen auch an kleinste Papierskulpturen denken, die sich aus dem weissen Papier herausgebildet haben. Dabei nehmen die willkürlichen Formen zuweilen fast gegenständliche, skulpturale Züge an, die sich trotz ihrer Brüchigkeit zu dreidimensionalen Projektionsflächen verdichten. In den Wandinstallationen

BURNING AIR
2010, DETAIL

Burning Air (2010/13, S. 17–19, 60) und *Brève braise* (2011, S. 58–59) erinnern verbrannte Seidenpapierstücke als Spuren an einen vergangenen Verbrennungsakt. Durch das Verbrennen wird das Seidenpapier in einen noch fragileren, irreversiblen Zustand überführt. Anschliessend bläst die Künstlerin die delikaten Stücke an die Wand, haucht ihnen so gleichsam wieder Leben ein, und zieht sich dann zurück. Im Laufe einer Ausstellung führen die dunklen Stücke ein durch den beim Vorbeigehen erzeugten Luftzug unabhängiges Eigenleben fort, indem sie, dürren Blättern gleich, kontinuierlich und zufällig zu Boden fallen und dort, wie kleine Aschehaufen, liegen bleiben. Während Asche normalerweise in einem Gefäss aufbewahrt wird, liegen die Stücke von *Burning Air* und *Brève braise* verstreut am Boden – ihrer Zerbrechlichkeit wird kein Schutz geboten. Die ephemeren Teile thematisieren Fragilität und Flüchtigkeit. Sie weisen damit eindringlich auf die Vergänglichkeit der Kunst und darüber hinaus des Lebens hin. Manon Bellet mutet uns existenzielle Fragen zu und unterläuft gleichzeitig den Ewigkeitsanspruch der Kunst. Die sich im ‚Moment des Falls' befindende Installation suggeriert jedoch alles andere als Leblosigkeit. Das stete Herabfallen der Seidenpapierstücke führt nicht nur zu einer Auslöschung der ursprünglichen Form, sondern ermöglicht Wandel und Erneuerung. Die Installation wird zu einem ephemeren Zeitbild, zum Schattenbild eines Augenblicks.

1 «Man muss sich nicht darüber sorgen, ob man forscht. Man muss nur wissen, dass das, was man macht, zu einem unerwarteten Ausgang führt» (George Brecht, Übersetzung der Autorin). Cf. dazu auch die Vernissagerede von Cornelia Dietschi Schmid, Kunstsammlung Hoffmann-La Roche, März 2010 (publiziert auf der Website von Manon Bellet).
2 Sybille Krämer, „Immanenz und Transzendenz der Spur: Über das epistemologische Doppelleben der Spur", in: *Spur. Spurenlesen als Orientierungstechnik und Wissenskunst*, hrsg. von Sybille Krämer, Werner Kogge und Gernot Grube, Frankfurt am Main: Suhrkamp, 2007, S. 155–181, hier S. 159.
3 Roland Barthes, *Mythen des Alltags*, (1957), Frankfurt am Main: Suhrkamp, 1996, S. 79.
4 Monika Wagner, *Das Material der Kunst. Eine andere Geschichte der Moderne*, München: C.H. Beck, 2001, S. 235.
5 Ebd.

incidence of burning and thus become "memory charged materials" with recollections inscribed into them. By suggesting a past fire they "become storage points,"[5] as Monika Wagner has put it in her study on the materials of Modernity. In *Burning Line* (2010–2011, pp. 62–63), for instance, charred edges are seen where tissue paper has been scorched. Depending on the intervention and the heat (which point to the carefully controlled use of fire), the traces of burning form variously sized positive and negative forms, which link up in "drawn" silhouettes. The charred edges are reminiscent of fine charcoal drawings, even although they were not created by the artist's hand but by the effects of fire. In the truest sense of the words these are in fact charcoal drawings. They also call to mind tiny paper sculptures that have formed from the white paper. At the same time these arbitrary forms take on an almost representational, sculptural air, which, despite their fragility, become three-dimensional projection surfaces. In the wall installations *Burning Air* (2010/13, pp. 17–19, 60) *Brève braise* (2011, pp. 58–59) scraps of burnt tissue paper recall a past moment of burning. Fire transposed the tissue paper into an even more delicate, irreversible state. At this point the artist then blew the flimsy scraps onto the wall, as though breathing life back into them, and then left the scene. During the course

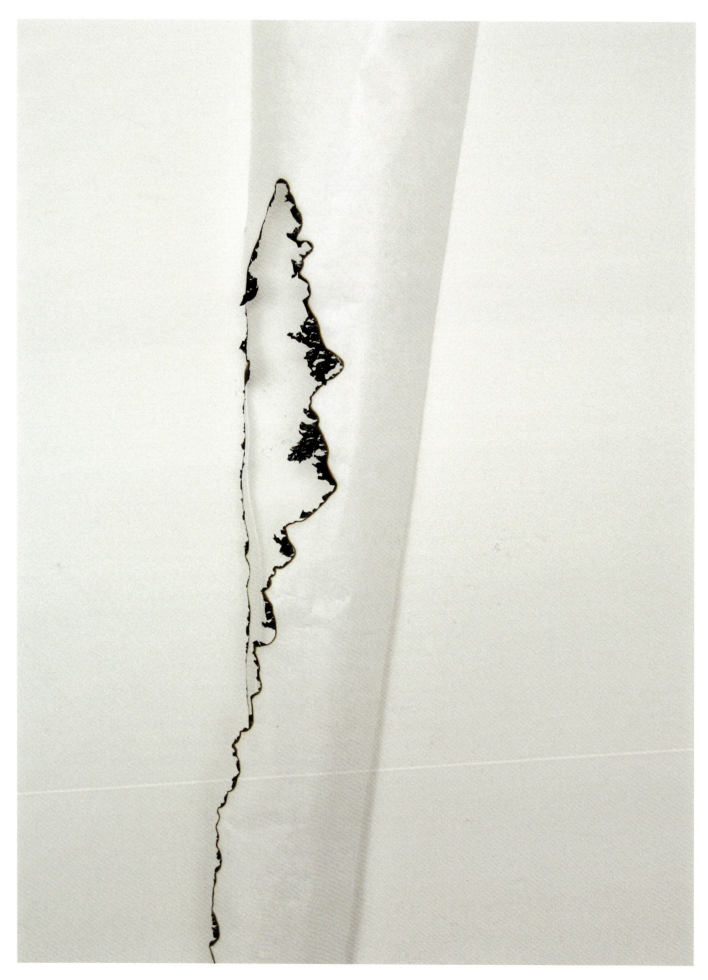

BURNING LINE
2010–2011, DETAIL

1. Cf. also the opening speech by Cornelia Dietschi Schmid, Kunstsammlung Hoffmann-La Roche, Basel, March 2010 (published on Manon Bellet's website).
2. Sybille Krämer, "Immanenz und Transzendenz der Spur: Über das epistemologische Doppelleben der Spur," in *Spur. Spurenlesen als Orientierungstechnik und Wissenskunst,* ed. by Sybille Krämer, Werner Kogge, and Gernot Grube, Frankfurt am Main: Suhrkamp, 2007, 155–81, here p. 159.
3. Roland Barthes on "Plastic" in *Mythologies,* selected and translated from the French by Annette Lavers, New York: Noonday Press, 1991, p. 97.
4. Monika Wagner, *Das Material der Kunst. Eine andere Geschichte der Moderne,* Munich: C.H. Beck, 2001, p. 235.
5. Ibid.

of the exhibition the dark pieces continued to "live" in the currents of air stirred by visitors walking by: like dry leaves they dropped randomly down onto the floor and remained where they had landed, forming tiny piles of ashes. Whereas ashes are normally contained in some kind of vessel, these insubstantial scraps lie scattered on the floor – with no protection. The ephemeral components of *Burning Air* and *Brève braise* point to fragility and volatility. They thus compellingly also point to the transience of art and ultimately of life, too. Manon Bellet confronts us with existential questions and, in so doing, undermines art's usual striving for permanence. Yet this installation, picturing the "moment of the fall," is far from an evocation of lifelessness. The constant fluttering downward of pieces of charred tissue paper is not about the destruction of the original form but about change and renewal. The installation is an ephemeral temporal image, a shadow picture of a moment.

BURNING LINE
2010–2011, DETAIL

"CROQUIS DE CHALEUR" ▶
2012–2013

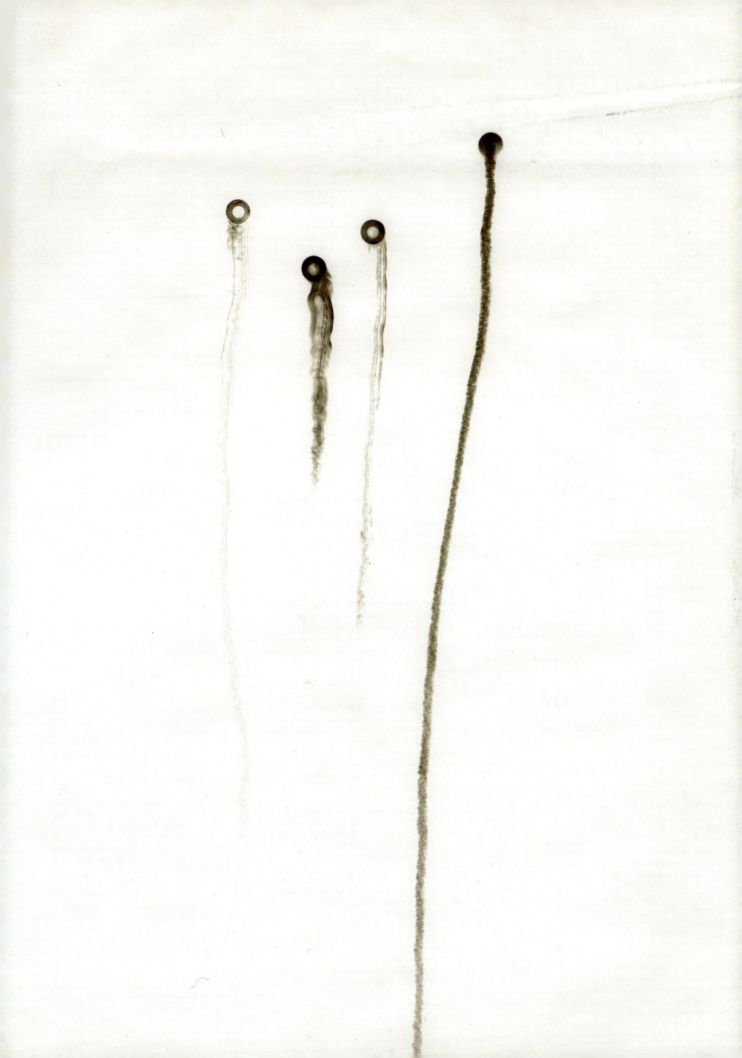

IDEAS IN PROCESS

Stéphanie Serra

Il n'y a pas de point fixe dans l'espace.
Merce Cunningham[1]

IDEAS IN PROCESS

Stéphanie Serra

There are no fixed points in space.
Merce Cunningham[1]

Manon Bellet est une âme vagabonde. Elle voyage. Elle respecte le flux naturel et constant du monde, son mouvement continu et perpétuel, et y prend part. C'est une observatrice, une chercheuse qui se plaît à mettre en place un processus et à observer son évolution, jusqu'à son autodestruction. Elle n'enferme pas les idées, mais les attrape pour mieux les relâcher: « Saisir une idée abstraite, la magnétiser, la faire apparaître […]. L'attraper avant qu'elle ne s'évapore, qu'elle ne change, qu'elle ne s'oublie, qu'elle ne s'efface, qu'elle ne chute »[2].

Elle peut ensuite décider d'inscrire l'idée ou la pensée dans un cahier sous forme de mots et la laisser là, le temps qu'elle devienne autre chose, un début d'œuvre peut-être, ou de la glisser sur une feuille volante, qui tombera et lui rendra sa liberté. L'idée peut aussi apparaître plus tard sous forme d'image ou d'empreinte, dans l'atelier, au travers de « croquis de chaleur » (2012–2013, pp. 64–71).

La tentative, de traduire un processus créatif à une date précise, de geler un équilibre en constante évolution est complexe et donc forcément simplifié. L'échelle n'y est pas respectée, mais le lien entre chaque phase du cycle de création est bien réel (cf. Creation Cycle, p. 76). Observer « l'avant » et « l'après » œuvre, la recontextualiser non pas dans son époque, mais dans son processus. Ne pas la voir comme une finalité mais comme un point sur une ligne continue.

Manon Bellet is a wandering soul. She travels. She respects the natural and constant flow of the world, its continuous and perpetual motion, and she participates in it. She is an observer, a researcher who enjoys setting up a process and observing its development, until the point at which it destroys itself. She does not imprison ideas, but rather catches them, the better to set them free: "Seize an abstract idea, magnetise it, make it appear […]. Catch it before it evaporates, before it changes, is forgotten, disappears, before it falls."[2]

She can then decide to record the idea or the thought in a notebook, in the form of words, and leave it there to become something else, the makings of a work, perhaps; or to slip it onto a loose sheet of paper which will one day fall and restore its freedom. The idea may also appear later in the form of an image or an imprint, in the studio as a "croquis de chaleur" (2012–2013, pp. 64–71).

The attempt to translate a creative process into a precise date, to freeze a balance that is in constant evolution, is both complex and, of necessity, simplified (cf. Creation Cycle, p. 76). The aim is to observe the "before" and "after" work, to recontextualise it not in its time, but in its process: to see it not as a finality, but rather as a point on a continuous line.

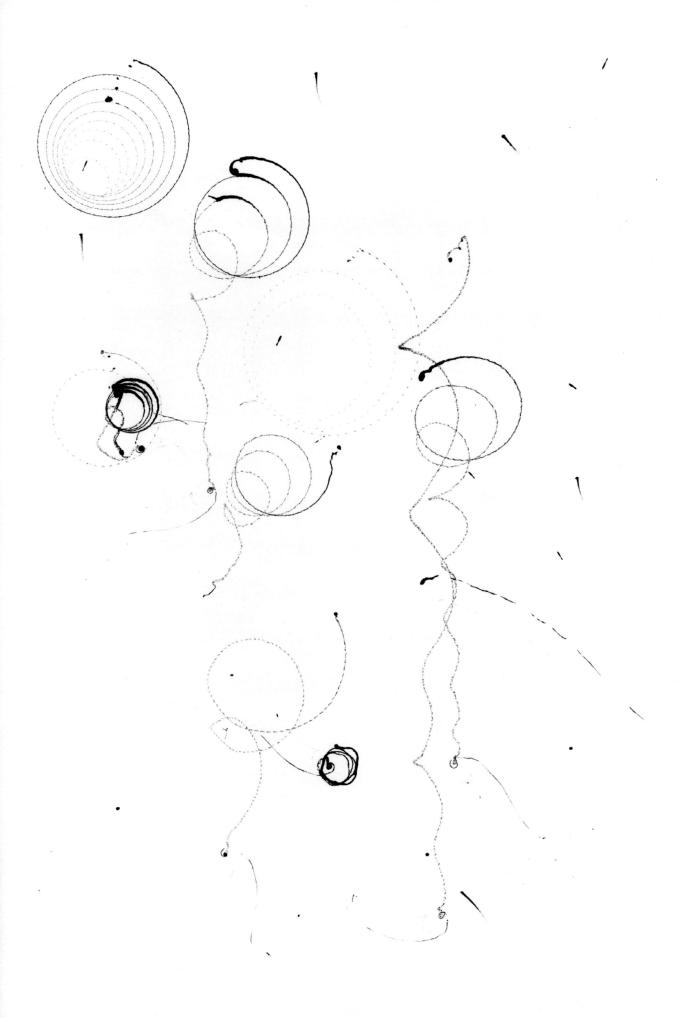

L'artiste oscille constamment entre des moments de confrontation avec le monde extérieur, où elle cherche des stimulations sonores, visuelles et sensorielles et son atelier – un espace plus introspectif – où elle alterne instants de réflexion, de calme, de lecture, d'écriture et de synthèse. Interface de méditation entre le monde et l'artiste, l'atelier est un espace fini ou elle essaie, par une discipline de travail, de provoquer l'état idéal qui lui permettra la création d'une œuvre. Hors de l'atelier, elle concentre ses impressions dans ses cahiers. Dans l'atelier, elle libère ensuite ses pensées aux travers de « croquis de chaleur » pour arriver dans une phase de flottement, ou l'espace est libre. Elle peut ainsi se confronter honnêtement avec la matière et l'expérimenter. Intervalle de possibles, ce moment de clarté fugace, n'aboutit pas forcement à une création d'œuvre mais incite à un nouveau tâtonnement. Et le cycle recommence.

Manon Bellet ne nie pas le mouvement continu du monde auquel elle prend part, elle l'intègre dans ses œuvres afin que celles-ci passent d'un immatériel à l'autre, rendant ces espaces de transition visibles, précieux et éphémères, ne laissant comme trace que le souvenir de l'idée capturée.

1   Merce Cunningham faisant référence à une remarque d'A. Einstein. *Merce Cunningham, le danseur et la danse, entretiens avec Jacqueline Lessehaeve,* trad. Jacqueline Lessehaeve, Paris: Pierre Belfond, 1988, p. 15.
2   Manon Bellet, échange de courriels avec l'auteur, 3 juin 2013.
3   Arthur Rimbaud, *Œuvres complètes,* Alchimie du verbe, Délire II, Une saison en enfer, établie et annotée par André Guyaux, Paris: Bibliothèque de la Pléiade, Gallimard, 2011, p. 263.
4   *William Kentridge, Cinq Thèmes au Jeu de Paume,* Paris: Jeu de Paume, Cinq Continents, 2010, p. 13.
5   Manon Bellet, échange de courriels avec l'auteur, 1er mai 2013.
6   Question adressée à Etel Adnan en référence au livre de Hubert Damisch, *Theorie du nuage,* Paris: Le Seuil, 1972, dans: Hans Ulrich Obrist, *Conversation avec Etel Adnan,* Paris: Manuella, 2012, p. 59.

1   Merce Cunningham referring to A. Einstein's remark. *Merce Cunningham, le danseur et la danse, entretiens avec Jacqueline Lessehaeve,* trans. Jacqueline Lessehaeve, Paris: Pierre Belfond, 1988, p. 15.
2   Manon Bellet, Email exchange with the author, 3 June 2013.
3   Arthur Rimbaud, *Œuvres complètes,* Alchimie du verbe, Délire II, Une saison en enfer, edited and annotated by André Guyaux, Paris: Bibliothèque de la Pléiade, Gallimard, 2011, p. 263.
4   *William Kentridge, Cinq Thèmes au Jeu de Paume,* Paris: Jeu de Paume, Cinq Continents, 2010, p. 13.
5   Manon Bellet, Email exchange with the author, 1 May 2013.
6   Question addressed to Etel Adnan referring to the book by Hubert Damisch, *Theorie du nuage,* Paris: Le Seuil, 1972, in Hans Ulrich Obrist, *Conversation avec Etel Adnan,* Paris: Manuella, 2012.

The artist moves constantly between moments of confrontation with the outside world where she seeks inspiration, be it heard, seen or felt; and times when she seeks refuge in her studio – a more introspective space – where she alternates between moments of reflection, calm, reading, writing and synthesis. An interface for meditation between the world and the artist, the studio is a finite space in which she endeavours, through disciplined work, to bring about the ideal state that will permit the creation of a work. Outside the studio, she condenses her impressions in her notebooks. In the studio, she then liberates her thoughts via "croquis de chaleur," thus entering a phase of drifting, where space is free: a state in which she can confront the material, honestly, face up to it and experiment with it. As a brief interval of possibility, this fleeting moment of clarity does not necessarily give rise to the creation of a work, but instead provides the impetus for a new, tentative quest, and the cycle begins again.

Manon Bellet does not deny the continuous movement of the world in which she is involved; rather, she integrates it into her works and so enables them to move from one immaterial state to another, rendering these transitional spaces visible, precious and ephemeral, leaving behind only the memory of the captured idea.

CREATION CYCLE

OUTSIDE THE STUDIO | **INSIDE THE STUDIO**

2. THE "CROQUIS DE CHALEUR"
Catching an image

Walking, thinking, stalking the image. Many of the hours spent in the studio are hours of walking, pacing back and forth across the space gathering the energy, the clarity to make the first mark. [...] *It is as if before the work can begin,* [...] *a different, invisible work must be done.* [...] *So my "fragments" are the product of internal thought processes, each completed fragment being the manifestation of the thoughts that occur to me and which I cast aside before work begins.*[4]
William Kentridge

Each morning in her studio, Manon Bellet begins by warming up: "I began drawing the "croquis de chaleur" on fax paper. I heat the metal tip that I use to draw on the thermal paper, causing lines, shapes and circles to appear. These drawings are a transition between my thought and the paper."[5]

In this moment of pleasure and play that precedes the possibility of creation, she produces free, spontaneous impressions with contours of black. An intermediate act that is essential yet invisible, the paper becomes a transitional object, a mediator between the outside world and the inside, capturing the image to free the thought. The free, unverbalised movement resonates with the studio space and the paper. In this daily performance dance that is similar to automatic writing, the artist brings about the state that will enable her to imagine a work free of self-censorship. When the traces appear, she paradoxically finds herself face to face with the blank paper, and ready to begin. Manon Bellet extracts and brings into being an imprint, an image. The mist clears, she can let go and make herself available to compose.

1. THE NOTEBOOKS
Catching an idea

I turned silences and nights into words. What was unutterable, I wrote down. I made the whirling world stand still.[3]
Arthur Rimbaud

Since the beginning of her artistic career, the artist has mixed fragments of thoughts, sounds and details of inspirations (quotations, photocopies of pages of books or covers, names of artists) with notes from everyday life (Post-It notes, telephone numbers, plans of exhibition galleries) which she archives in black notebooks. This concentration of scraps of information acts as a kind of organised and reassuring chaos, where a thought has been captured on a given date. As still location for the conjunction of her chosen ideas, they operate without system or conclusion, existing instead like butterfly nets capturing ideas and thoughts in flight. Their rhythm comes from their breathing (blank pages) and periods of lesser or greater activity.

To prevent ideas from being locked in, and to allow them to maintain their own life, the artist inserts loose sheets held by magnets and, on the reverse, iron filings. Over time, this causes the appearance of small drawn patches that move around the sheets then become demagnetised, falling down and, in so doing, causing the sheet to fall down too, taking with it the idea that it contained.

3. THE WORKS
Creating, then allowing to evolve

It's a paradox: how can one paint a cloud if it is impossible to grasp?[6]
Hans Ulrich Obrist

How to concentrate something fluid and yet let it remain free? Through her choice of materials and ideas, the artist sets up a proposition, a possibility of success or failure that she defines in order to let it evolve. Like free ideas, which leave, come back and then fly away, the work is not intended to be eternal but to transform itself and move, like any living organism or any flow. It attempts to conserve the uncertain.

Objet et Sujet → trai...
Comme écrire un livre ...
Neuroscience, neu...
Le dessin du li...
→ sphère
un texte b...
→ dessin

Le battement d'aile
d'un papillon.

La vie n'a pas de sens intrin...
il faut lui inventer un
sens
La vie repose sur cette invention de
sens
La civilisation indienne
→ National / croyance.
Travail / prière

14H
rue diderot

Nomanache Abha Dawesar "Sensorium"

...personne / penser à la ... Personne   Laïla
...distance   d'ivresar
                                         Écrit 10/18

... → Toile d'araigné / Angle l'Adés.

... deux côté du Cerveau
... totalité de chose que l'on peut savoir
dans tous les sens.   Edit
... croquis par la ... formé par les   061 322 3247
humans.
... bonne façon de vie
... nature de son art quelque chose de
                       Fondamental.

...angues multiple → perpectives différentes.

...oman sur le Temps
Temps cyclique   chrétien
       Orion   occidan.

...flèche du Temps   uroboros grecque
Flèche droite, ... plume d'un écrivain.

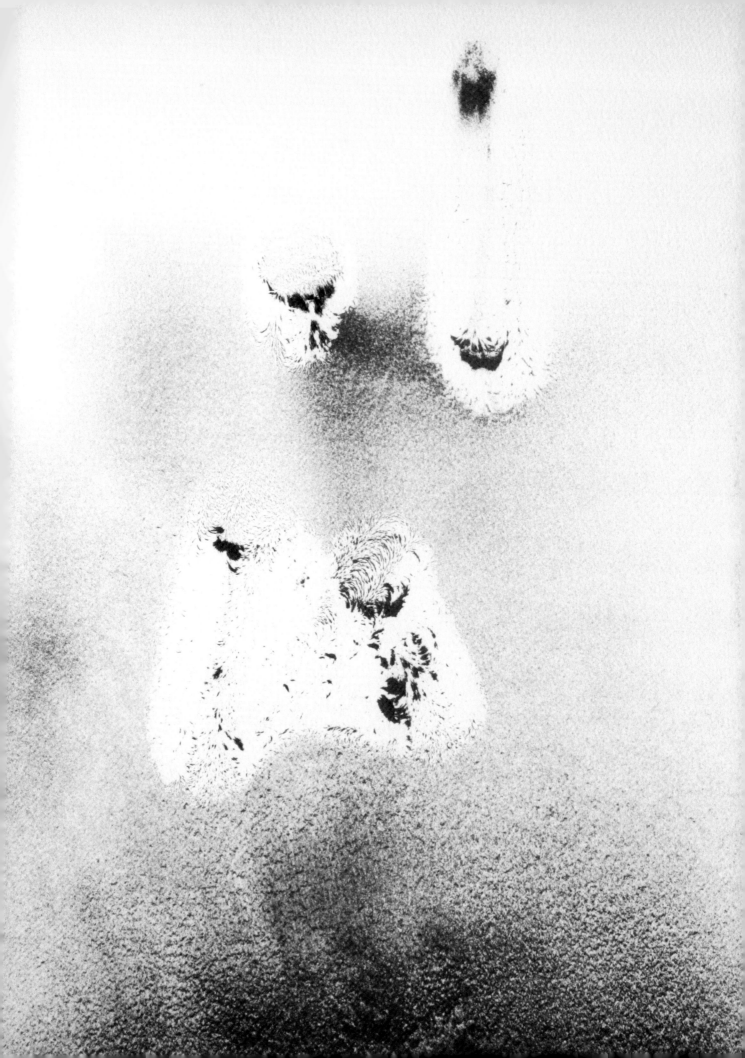

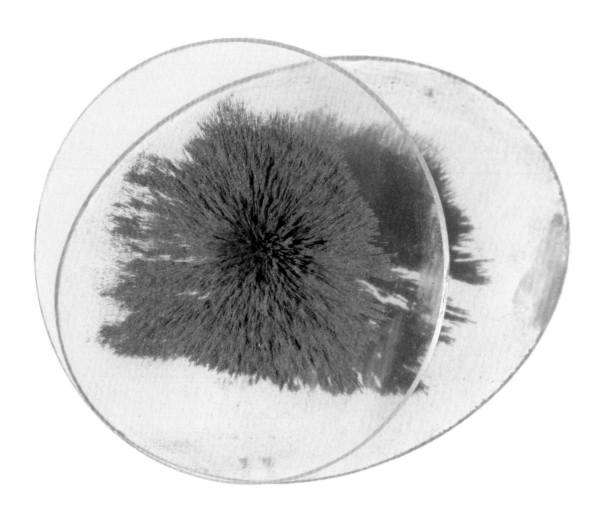

JOUER AVEC LE FEU

Manon Bellet, en conversation avec
Mathieu Copeland

PLAYING WITH FIRE

**Manon Bellet in conversation with
Mathieu Copeland**

◀◀◀ ENSEMBLE D'UN ÉCLAT
2013

◀◀ UNTITLED
2013

◀ BRILLURE
2011

MATHIEU COPELAND : De ton travail, tu dis essayer de rendre les moments de transition précieux. J'aimerais comprendre ce que tu entends par « précieux » : est-ce que cela fait référence au matériel utilisé, comme la feuille d'or ou le papier de soie, ou s'agit-il plutôt du soin particulièrement soutenu ou « précieux » que tu accordes à cette étape du processus de création ?

MANON BELLET : Ce serait plutôt la seconde proposition. Je me réfère ici à une étape difficilement perceptible au moment où l'on voit l'œuvre présentée dans l'exposition. Je pense à ces moments relativement intimes d'atelier où l'œuvre est en devenir. De ces intervalles, que je vis seule dans le développement du travail, de ce mouvement constant où je vois le médium se transformer physiquement, si l'on peut dire, avant que l'œuvre ne s'achève. C'est ce mouvement de transition « précieux » que j'essaie de « retenir » et de retranscrire dans l'œuvre finale.

COPELAND : Cela revient à ce que tu entends comme la mise à nu de l'œuvre ? Il me semble qu'une des questions fondamentales serait « où situer l'œuvre ».

BELLET : Pour moi, l'œuvre se situe précisément dans cet entre-deux, au moment de la chute.

COPELAND : Ce qui revient à cet énoncé radical, lorsque tu affirmes que l'intention est plus importante que le résultat. La chute, ainsi que ce refus de résultat, induit une attention toute particulière au travail en train de se faire. Cela me rappelle ce que disait Jérôme Bel : il citait, en parlant de l'idée d'échec, la phrase de William

MATHIEU COPELAND: You say that your work is about making moments of transition precious. I'd like to understand what you mean by "precious": is it a reference to the material you use, the gold leaf or the tissue paper; or is it more to do with the particularly sustained, "precious" care that you take with that stage in the creative process?

MANON BELLET: It's more the second idea. What I'm referring to is a stage that's difficult to perceive when you see the work displayed in an exhibition. I'm thinking of those relatively intimate moments in the studio when the work is in the process of becoming: those brief periods which I experience alone as the work develops; the constant motion in which I can see the medium transforming itself physically, as one might say, before the work is complete. It's that "precious" movement of transition that I try to "capture" and retranscribe in the final work.

COPELAND: So it comes down to what you see as "stripping the work bare"? It seems to me that one of the fundamental questions is where to locate the work.

BELLET: For me, the work is located precisely in that in-between state, in the moment when it falls.

COPELAND: Which brings us back to your radical affirmation that the intention is more important than the result. That falling, like this rejection of the completed product,

Forsythe « le ballet est une philosophie de l'échec ». Une phrase qui fait elle-même écho à cette autre phrase célèbre de Samuel Beckett « try again, fail again, fail better » [« essayer encore, échouer encore, échouer mieux »].

BELLET : Et la chute fait rebondir sur autre chose. Cette matière stimulante qui donne vie à l'œuvre, qui donnera naissance à quelque chose d'autre, de visuel ou de mental. Cela ne s'arrête jamais !

COPELAND : Ainsi, la chute est-elle d'abord un mouvement de matière, ou un travail de « sculpture » ?

BELLET : La chute découle d'un mouvement plus chorégraphique que sculptural. Mais dans certains cas elle peut induire aussi le façonnage d'une matière. Si l'on parle de sculpture, dans ce cas elle pourrait suggérer « la chute du corps de l'œuvre … »

COPELAND : Et toujours en cherchant à mettre des mots sur le travail que tu mets en œuvre, serait-il correct de dire que tes dessins ont finalement un aspect plus sculptural que pictural ?

BELLET : Les « croquis de chaleur » (2012–2013, pp. 64–71), dessinés sur papier thermique avec des pointes de métal chaudes sont pour moi une transition entre le lieu où j'élabore le travail – le studio et l'espace d'exposition avant la réalisation *in situ* de l'œuvre. Dans l'exécution des travaux *in situ,* il s'agit d'un rapport physique au lieu, d'une prise de risque vis-à-vis de l'espace d'exposition spécifique à ce moment de la réalisation. Il m'est donc impossible d'avoir en continu ce rapport physique à l'espace dans mon atelier. Ces « croquis » relèvent pour moi de la

creates a particular focus on the work as it is being made. It reminds me of something Jérôme Bel said about failure: he quoted William Forsythe's phrase, "ballet is a philosophy of failure." That in turn echoes another famous comment by Samuel Beckett: "try again, fail again, fail better."

BELLET: And that fall sends you back to something else: the stimulating material that gives life to the work, and that will give birth to something different, something visual or mental. It's never-ending!

COPELAND: So is the fall first and foremost a movement of the material or a work of "sculpture"?

BELLET: The fall derives from a movement that is more choreographic than sculptural. But in certain cases it can also give rise to a shaping of the material. If we are talking of sculpture, in this case it might suggest the "fall of the work's body".

COPELAND: If I can try again to put into words what you do, would it be correct to say that your drawings are ultimately more sculptural than pictorial?

BELLET: The "croquis de chaleur" (2012–2013, pp. 64–71), drawn on thermal paper with hot metal tips are, for me, a transition between the place where I execute the work – the studio – and the exhibition space before the work is realised *in situ*. When work is carried out *in situ,* there

is a physical relationship with the place. You're taking a risk against the exhibition space specifically at that moment of realisation. It is therefore not possible for me to maintain this kind of continuous physical relationship in my studio. For me, these "sketches" are a kind of choreography. They allow me to move within a space in a small format. That transfigures the blank space of the sheet of paper, the studio space, or indeed the mental space. The fact that everything is hot, and that I have to handle the tools in a certain way, results in movements that are different from traditional drawing. I'm "playing with fire," but in an extremely controlled way. I try to be surprised by the work. How should I reconcile that with the fact that the drawing instrument is burning? What interests me is the way in which I adapt to the situation, just as the work adapts to the medium that I am using.

COPELAND: We're close here to the way in which Gustav Metzger made his series of *Plotter Drawings* in 1970: he used a light pen on photosensitive paper, controlled by a computer, and he got first the artist Heather Peri and then the academic D. E. Evans to produce a "light drawing." In your case the photographic process is similar: the heat on this photosensitive or carbon paper generates this design which is a comment on the act of writing, and thus renders it present.

UNTITLED
2012

JALOUSIE D'HIER
2012

JALOUSIE D'HIER
2012, DETAIL

chorégraphie. Ils me permettent, sur petit format, de bouger dans un espace. Cela transfigure le blanc de la feuille, l'espace de l'atelier, ou encore l'espace mental. Le fait que tout soit chaud, que je doive manipuler les instruments d'une certaine manière, tout cela induit des gestes différents que ceux du dessin traditionnel. Je « joue avec le feu », mais de manière extrêmement contrôlée. Je cherche à être surprise par l'œuvre. Comment composer avec le fait que l'outil du dessin soit brûlant ? Ce qui m'intéresse, c'est la manière dont je m'adapte à la situation, tout comme l'œuvre s'adapte au medium que j'utilise.

COPELAND : En cela, nous sommes proches de la manière dont Gustav Metzger développe en 1970 sa série de *Plotter Drawing*. À l'aide d'un stylex lumineux sur papier photosensible, contrôlé informatiquement, Metzger fait réaliser dans un premier temps par une artiste, Heather Peri, puis par l'universitaire D. E. Evans, un « dessin de lumière ». Dans ton cas le procédé photographique est similaire, la chaleur, sur ce papier photosensible ou carbone, génère ce dessin qui commente le geste d'écriture, et le rend ainsi présent.

BELLET : J'utilise le potentiel du matériel. Dans le cas de la série *Taches aveugles* (2012, pp. 27–29), où le centre de la feuille du papier carbone a été brûlé de manière circulaire, le papier carbone contient de l'encre. Faire ce trou par la brûlure amène une tache par l'absence. Plutôt que révéler ce qui est contenu, la chaleur le fait disparaître. Et dans le cas des dessins sur papier thermique

BELLET: I exploit the potential of the material. In the *Taches aveugles* (2012, pp. 27–29) series, where the centre of the sheet of carbon paper was burnt in a circular pattern, the carbon paper contains ink. Making the hole by burning creates a mark through absence. Instead of revealing what is inside, the heat makes it disappear. With the drawings on thermal paper, the opposite happens: the heat makes the mark appear. It is an attempt to capture something in the instant of a gesture, which is intended to be transformed.

COPELAND: When I look at your burnt paper works, the sheets with a burn in their centre, and the rolls of thermal paper with heat marks, their fundamental instability reminds me of the work of the artist David Medalla. Medalla is currently working on self-eliminating "erasable drawings." He once observed to me that given the quantity of works of art that are constantly being produced, one might as well make drawings that erased themselves. Unlike the famous *Bubble Machines* sculptures – columns of bubbles that, although they burst and vanish, constantly generate that formless sculpture – these drawings will never come back. It seems to me that this same constant impermanence, this disappearance, can also be found in your work.

BELLET: That's because I want to avoid fixing time. Their

c'est l'inverse qui se passe, la chaleur fait apparaître le trait. Il s'agit d'une tentative de capturer quelque chose dans l'instantané d'un geste, qui est destiné à être transformé.

COPELAND : Au vu de tes œuvres de papiers calcinés, de tes feuilles brûlées en leur centre, ou encore de ces rouleaux et feuilles thermiques marqués par la chaleur, ces pièces fondamentalement instables me font penser à l'œuvre de l'artiste David Medalla. Medalla travaille actuellement à des « erasable drawings », des dessins qui s'effacent eux-mêmes. À leurs propos, Medalla me disait qu'au de la quantité d'œuvres d'art constamment réalisées, pourquoi ne pas faire des dessins qui s'effaceraient eux-mêmes. À l'opposé de ces fameuses sculptures de *Bubble Machines* – ces colonnes de bulles qui, bien qu'elles éclatent et disparaissent, génèrent constamment cette sculpture informe –, ces dessins eux ne reviendront jamais. Il me semble retrouver dans ton travail cette constante impermanence, cette disparition.

BELLET : C'est pour éviter de fixer un temps. Leur transformation constante permet de ne jamais les figer. Et ce n'est pas seulement une disparition, car constamment, quelque chose d'autre apparaît. Comme Medalla le suggère dans ces dessins qui disparaissent, nous sommes face à une abondance d'images. Et dans cet environnement, visuellement très riche et complexe, je trouve qu'il est problématique de produire des œuvres figées. C'est donc pour moi à chaque fois un challenge de mettre en place de nouveaux procédés pour permettre à mes œuvres d'être en constante

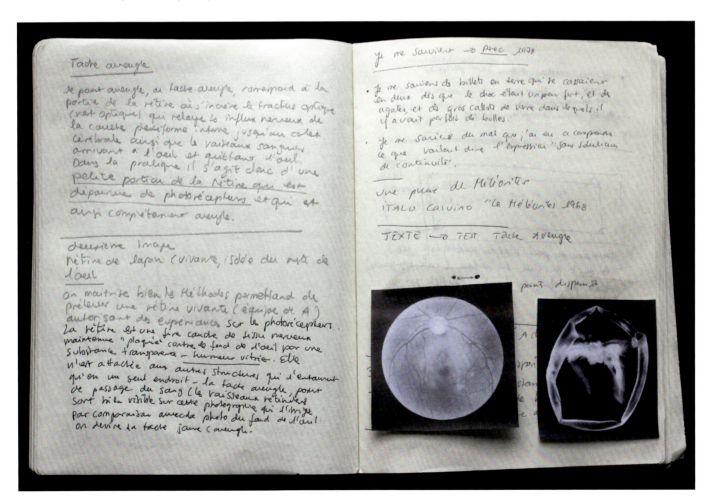

métamorphose et de déclencher, par la même occasion, de nouvelles pistes de lecture de mon travail.

COPELAND : Nous pouvons penser à une double disparition, une disparition immédiate de l'objet par sa brûlure puis, une fois passé le moment de son exposition, une seconde disparition lors de sa mise au rebut. La seule chose qui perdure est ce principe de réalisation, des partitions que tu exécutes. Revenons ainsi à cette idée de la destruction. Brûler est un acte essentiel de la destruction. Qu'il s'agisse de l'autodafé, de la purification par le feu … Nous pourrions convier nombre de philosophies et de pratiques artistiques de la destruction. Je pense évidemment à Gustav Metzger, et à son Manifeste pour un *Art Auto-Destructif* écrit en 1959, à John Latham et ses *SKOOB Towers,* ces piles de livres auxquelles il mettait le feu ; à Niki de Saint-Phalle et à ses œuvres réalisées en tirant dessus avec un fusil ; aux *Shotgun Paintings* de William S. Burroughs – ces œuvres de la fin des années 1980 réalisées à la carabine ; à la *Shooting Gallery,* cette proposition dessinée par Làszlò Moholy-Nagy en 1925, invitant les spectateurs à tirer sur les œuvres, etc. Toutes amènent cette pensée d'un acte de violence générant l'œuvre.

BELLET : L'acte de destruction généré par la création de l'œuvre est un acte violent, mais le résultat est quant à lui apaisant. Nous pourrions le réduire à la violence d'un geste créateur, tout comme l'on parle de la violence d'un mot, ou d'une idée. Le contact physique ou les paroles sont ici remplacées par l'acte créateur de l'œuvre. La majorité des papiers calcinés se détériore, alors que le papier de

constant transformation means I can avoid immobilising them. And it's not just about disappearance: something else is always appearing. As Medalla suggests in his disappearing drawings, we are faced with an abundance of images. In that visually rich and complex environment, I think it is problematic to produce works that are immobilised. So for me it's a challenge each time to set up new procedures so that my works can be in constant metamorphosis and, at the same time, open up new ways of reading my work.

COPELAND: What we have here is a kind of dual disappearance: the immediate disappearance of the object as it burns and, once the time of its exhibition has past, a second disappearance when it is discarded. The only thing that lasts is this principle of realisation, the scores that you create. Let's come back to this idea of destruction. Burning is an essential act of destruction. We can think in terms of *auto-da-fé* – purification by fire; we can compile a list of philosophies and artistic practices of destruction. I am of course thinking of Gustav Metzger, and the manifesto of *Auto-Destructive Art* that he wrote in 1959; of John Latham and his *SKOOB Towers,* the piles of books that he set fire to; of Niki de Saint-Phalle and the works she made by firing a gun at them; of William S. Burroughs and his *Shotgun Paintings* from the late 1980s; of the

soie – le seul papier que je brûle – reste sous sa forme d'origine, même après sa combustion. Léger, il se consume rapidement. Néanmoins, je n'envisage pas cela comme un acte de destruction, mais comme une transformation. La destruction n'est jamais complète. Il s'agit de tirer à l'essence du matériau. Les papiers sont brûlés, puis je les souffle sur un mur apprêté.

COPELAND : Dans une installation de papiers de soie brûlés, collés au mur, il n'y a qu'une inscription temporaire de l'œuvre. Avec le temps, les papiers se décollent, puis finissent au sol, pour être finalement débarrassé. Comment envisager le futur de cette œuvre ?

BELLET : Il y a ce « presque rien » … Les feuilles brûlées vont ensuite chuter. Le mur sera repeint … Par leur désintégration, mes pièces en papier brûlé sont encore comme un symbole possible de l'échec, qu'il m'intéresse aussi de questionner. Un échec qui, encore un fois, est exploité dans le bon sens et donne à chaque fois naissance à autre chose. Un peu comme dans la science et la technologie, lorsque, à chaque nouvelle invention, l'ancienne hypothèse devient obsolète. La nature de l'œuvre est en constant devenir …

COPELAND : Il est fascinant d'envisager les aspects temporels qui sont au cœur d'un travail. Ainsi, j'aurais voulu envisager avec toi l'opposé du caractère éphémère du papier brûlé, pour discuter de l'apparente permanence de la porcelaine.

BELLET : Cela m'est venu de la nécessité d'installer une œuvre *in situ* pour une collection privée (*Plis sûrs,* 2012, pp. 99–101). Séduits par une installation de papiers brûlés, des collectionneurs désiraient

Shooting Gallery, that proposition designed by László Moholy-Nagy in 1925, inviting spectators to fire at the works, and so on. All of them convey that idea of an act of violence creating the work.

BELLET: The act of destruction engendered by the creation of the work is a violent act, but the result is soothing. We could bring down to the violence of a creative gesture, just as one speaks of the violence of a word, or an idea. Here, physical contact or words are replaced by the creative act of the work. The majority of the charred papers deteriorate, but the tissue paper – the only paper that I burn – remains in its original form even after it has been burnt. It is light and so is consumed rapidly. Nevertheless, I see this not as an act of destruction but rather as a transformation. The destruction is never complete. It's about drawing out the essence of the material. The papers are burnt, and then I blow them onto a prepared wall.

COPELAND: In an installation of burnt tissue paper glued to a wall the work is only recorded temporarily. With time, the papers come unstuck and end up on the floor, where they are finally disposed of. What kind of a future can this work have?

BELLET: There is that "next to nothing" … The burnt papers will fall down at some point. The wall will be repainted… In their disintegration, my burnt paper works are like a

une version permanente de l'œuvre. J'ai ainsi cherché à les retranscrire de manière interposée, par un matériau noble et fragile, rappelant cette chute possible. Ces feuilles, aspirées au plafond, donnent l'impression de tomber. Elles sont figées, mais parlent, au final, de la même chose.
COPELAND : Ce serait si beau qu'elles tombent et se brisent !
BELLET : Le temps nous le dira ! Elles posent des questions quant à la validité de l'œuvre. Comment s'approprier une œuvre, dans quelle mesure je suis prête à accepter cela, etc.
COPELAND : Et ce sans regret ?
BELLET : Sans aucun regret ! Cela m'a permis de développer des recherches sur la porcelaine, ainsi que d'envisager mes œuvres dans un contexte privé et domestique.
COPELAND : On en revient à cette pensée du « moment » de l'œuvre. Une solution possible aurait été de donner à ces collectionneurs une instruction pour réaliser des papiers brûlés, comme une chorégraphie ou un rituel à réaliser chaque jour. L'œuvre réside-t-elle dans l'énoncé de sa partition ?
BELLET : Oui, et pourtant, au travers de cette technique qui paraît si simple, il y a le plaisir de le faire soi-même. Dans ce cas la question se pose de savoir s'il serait pour moi envisageable de ne proposer que la matière du travail (les papiers de soie, le feu et la colle) pour avoir l'essence de l'œuvre.
COPELAND : C'est cette possibilité d'osciller entre l'aléatoire et le figé. En envisageant tes travaux avec les papiers thermiques, ces

possible symbol of failure, which I am also interested in questioning. It's a failure that, once again, is exploited in the good sense of the word, and every time gives birth to something new; rather as, in science and technology, each new invention renders the old hypothesis obsolete. The nature of the work is in a constant state of becoming.
COPELAND: It's fascinating to consider the temporal aspects that are at the heart of a work. For instance, I'd like to look at the opposite of the ephemeral nature of burnt paper and discuss the apparent permanence of porcelain.
BELLET: That came to me as a result of the need to install a work *in situ* for a private collection (*Plis sûrs,* 2012, pp. 99–101). The collectors had been attracted by a burnt paper installation and wanted a permanent version of the work. So I tried to retranscribe them in an intermediate way, using a material that was noble and fragile, recalling the possibility of downfall. Those sheets, adhering the ceiling, give the impression of falling. They are frozen and yet ultimately they are approaching the same thing.
COPELAND: It would be so marvellous if they fell down and broke!
BELLET: Time will tell! They ask questions about the validity of the work: how to appropriate it, how far I'm prepared to accept that, and so on.
COPELAND: So you have no regrets?

PLIS SÛRS
2012, DETAIL

BELLET: None at all! It was a chance to do some research into porcelain, and to see how my works look in a private, domestic context.

COPELAND: That brings us back to this idea of the "moment" of the work. You could perhaps have given the collectors instructions on how to make burnt papers, like a choreography or a ritual to be performed each day. Does the work reside in the wording of its score?

BELLET: Yes, and yet through that seemingly simple technique you have the pleasure of doing it yourself. In this case, it's a question of knowing whether I could contemplate supplying only the working materials (the tissue papers, the fire and the glue) and thereby preserve the essence of the work.

COPELAND: It's a chance to move between the random and the fixed. When we look at your works with thermal paper, these rolls of fax paper (*Sans titre sans encre*, 2010, pp. 2–4, 102, 104–105), we are tempted to think that in absolute terms, they exist only for a given time. Because they are photosensitive they never cease evolving towards inevitable destruction.

BELLET: They darken over time. As they brown, the papers try in vain to reveal a certain visual material that is subject to the passing of time. They are at once ephemeral and very physical.

rouleaux de fax, on en vient à penser que dans l'absolu, ceux-ci n'existent que pour un temps donné. Etant photosensibles, ils ne cessent d'évoluer, vont vers une destruction inévitable (*Sans titre sans encre,* 2010, pp. 2–4, 102, 104–105).

BELLET : Ils se foncent avec le temps. Ces papiers brunissant essayent vainement de donner à voir une certaine matière visuelle soumise au temps qui s'écoule. Ils sont à la fois éphémères et très physiques.

COPELAND : Cette pensée de l'éphémère me ramène à Wu Tzao Tang, le grand artiste chinois de la dynastie des Tang. Il est considéré comme l'un des plus grands artistes de son époque, bien qu'aucune de ses œuvres ne nous soit parvenue. Son œuvre nous est pourtant accessible par des copies et des gravures, comme ce portrait de Confucius. À cette première disparition, s'ajoute le mythe de sa mort. L'histoire veut que Wu Tzao Tang fasse venir l'empereur pour voir l'œuvre murale que ce dernier lui avait commandée. Parmi les nombreux et riches éléments de nature peints au mur du palais se trouvent l'entrée d'une cave. L'artiste frappe dans ces mains et la grotte peinte s'ouvre. Il y entre, la cave se referme soudainement derrière lui. Il disparaît à jamais, tout comme sa peinture qui s'efface instantanément, laissant l'empereur abasourdi. Au-delà de cette allégorie souvent citée, je m'intéresse à cette double disparition. Dans ton travail nous ne sommes pas dans ce qui est apparemment détruit et donné à voir dans un premier temps, mais dans ce qui va advenir de la pièce.

SANS TITRE SANS ENCRE
2010, DETAIL

BELLET: Cela me fait penser à cette phrase de Paul Valéry, «voir, c'est oublier le nom de ce que l'on voit»[1], à cet autre temps, qu'est celui de la musique: je pense aux sensations physiques que suggère Eliane Radigue dans son œuvre sonore, à ses pièces intitulées *Adnos* de 1973, réalisées sur magnétophone à bandes. J'ai eu la chance de les entendre dans une rediffusion de son œuvre au Festival CTM de Berlin en 2012. Entendre cette musique, dans une salle obscure et sans aucune personne sur scène[2], la matière du son modelant l'espace vide, m'a beaucoup stimulée. C'est un acte de performance. Je pense aussi au musicien Stephen O'Malley. J'aime le rapport de son corps avec son instrument, sa manière de jouer avec ses amplificateurs. Je m'intéresse à l'attirance du son: sa violence crée une résonance corporelle, comme sur une membrane d'où se dégage ce calme paradoxal, une sensualité. Cette modification constante mêle la rapidité et l'instantané. Ce lent étirement du son en devient méditatif.

COPELAND: Pourrais-tu envisager la présentation de tes œuvres sous forme de performance?

BELLET: Ce qui m'intéresse est ce qu'il en advient, et non de dévoiler le processus.

COPELAND: Est-il donc juste de penser que le moment de l'œuvre débute avec sa présentation?

BELLET: Il m'est difficile de déterminer précisément le moment où l'œuvre est terminée, mais il est juste de penser qu'elle s'achève lors de sa présentation. Cela vaut en particulier pour les travaux

COPELAND: That idea of the ephemeral brings me back to Wu Tzao Tang, the great Chinese artist of the Tang Dynasty. He is considered one of the greatest artists of his time, even though none of his works have come down to us. Yet his work is accessible to us via copies and engravings such as this portrait of Confucius. As well as that first disappearance there is the myth surrounding his death. The story goes that Wu Tzao Tang invites the emperor to view the mural that the emperor has commissioned from him. Among the many, rich elements of nature painted on the wall of the palace is the entrance to a cave. The artist claps his hands and the painted grotto opens. He enters, and the cave suddenly closes up behind him. He disappears for ever, just like his painting, which immediately erases itself, leaving the emperor stunned. Beyond the often-cited allegory, I'm interested in that dual disappearance. In your work, we're dealing not with what is apparently destroyed and revealed at the outset, but rather with what the piece will become.

BELLET: That remains me of what Paul Valéry said, "to see is to forget the name of what one is seeing,"[1] and also of that other time, which is the time of music: I'm thinking of the physical sensations that Eliane Radigue suggests in her sound work, and her *Adnos* of 1973, which were made on a tape recorder. I had the opportunity to

SANS TITRE SANS ENCRE
2010

sur papier fax ou papier de soie brûlé, qui changent constamment durant leur présentation. Bien qu'inévitablement leur devenir soit de périr et de chuter. Mes œuvres chutent sur le mur, sur le papier ou encore dans l'espace même d'exposition et, métaphoriquement, donnent à voir le glissement des idées et leurs évolutions constantes. J'aime l'idée «du moment de l'œuvre» car cela la rattache à un temps précis.

COPELAND: Après avoir envisagé la temporalité de l'œuvre, j'aimerais revenir à ce que serait le lieu de l'œuvre.

BELLET: Il n'est pas facile pour moi de déterminer un lieu fixe, il s'agit, à mon avis, de différents lieux. Mais si je devais m'arrêter à l'un d'eux, se serait celui de la pensée. En m'appuyant sur les mots de l'artiste et écrivaine Etel Adnan, qui dit que son cerveau est un laboratoire alchimique, un outil capable de transmuter les événements pour en extraire la substantifique moelle[3]. Pour moi l'œuvre débute réellement dans la pensée. Il s'agit ensuite de la traduire matériellement dans l'espace. C'est à ce moment seulement que je parviens, paradoxalement, à envisager une œuvre de plus en plus immatérielle et que je prends conscience de la réduction possible de mon travail. Par le son et l'écriture notamment, la vibration des mots et leur potentiel sonore. Ce qui me permettrait plus librement de faire bouger l'œuvre d'un lieu à l'autre.

COPELAND: Des mots que l'on retrouve inscrits non pas tant sur le papier brûlé, mais au travers de ta manière de nommer les œuvres. L'appellation de tes pièces oscille entre poésie, romantisme et jeu

hear them when her work was repeated as part of the CTM Festival in Berlin in 2011. Hearing that music in a dark room and with no-one on the stage,[2] and with the sound as matter shaping the empty space, was something I found very stimulating. It's an act of performance. I also think of the musician Stephen O'Malley. I like the relationship between his body and his instrument, and the way he works with his amplifiers. I'm interested in the attraction of sound: the violence of the sound creates a resonance within the body, as if on a membrane from which a paradoxical calm emanates, a kind of sensuality. This constant change mixes rapidity and instantaneity. The slow elongation of the sound becomes meditative.

COPELAND: Could you imagine presenting your works as a performance?

BELLET: What interests me is what comes out of them, not revealing the process.

COPELAND: So is it true to say that the work's moment begins with its presentation?

BELLET: It's difficult for me to say exactly when the work is finished, but it is certainly the case that it is completed when it is presented. That's especially true of the works on fax paper or burnt tissue paper, which change constantly while they are being presented. Even though their inevitable fate is to perish and fall. My works fall from

the wall, from the paper or indeed in the exhibition space itself and metaphorically reveal the shifting of ideas and their constant evolutions. I like the idea of the "moment of the work," because that attaches it to a specific time.
COPELAND: Now that we've considered the temporal aspect of the work, I'd like to come back to where its location might be.
BELLET: It's not easy for me to settle on a single place; I believe a number are involved. But if I had to choose one of them, it would be the place of the thought. I'm guided by the words of the artist and writer Etel Adnan, who says that her brain is an alchemist's laboratory, a tool that can transmute events so as to extract their essence.[3] For me, the work really begins in the thought. The next step

de mots. Un énoncé aussi littéral que distancié vis-à-vis des pièces elles-mêmes.

BELLET: Poser un titre sur une œuvre revient à poser une œuvre sur le mur. C'est déjà la définir et lui donner des pistes de lecture. Ces titres en donnent, mais ces pistes de lecture sont souvent inexactes.

COPELAND: Les titres, à l'image de tes pièces, semblent temporaires, transitoires et instables. S'agit-il d'autant de façon de t'effacer?

BELLET: Tout à fait. Tout comme cette série d'autoportraits qui ne sont rien d'autres que des projections d'ombres abstraites de mon corps sur une peinture (*Le rideau dans le tableau*, 2009, pp. 107/109). Mais il est vain de penser que ce n'est qu'effacement. Ce qui me stimule c'est de chercher comment apparaître.

1 Michel Philippon : « Paul Valéry, une poétique en poèmes », Bordeaux: Presses universitaires de Bordeaux, 1993.
2 Le parti-pris d'Eliane Radigue étant de ne jamais apparaître sur scène et d'installer tout le système technique en coulisse, la scène ne contenant que les amplificateurs.
3 Hans Ulrich Obrist, *Conversation avec Etel Adnan*, Paris: Manuella, 2012, p. 27.

---

is to translate it materially into space. It's only then that, paradoxically, I am able to envisage a piece that is more and more immaterial and become aware of the ways I can reduce my work: through sound and writing, in particular, the vibration of the words and their sound potential. And that would enable me to shift the work from one place to another more freely.

COPELAND: Words that are recorded not so much on the paper, which is burnt, but through your way of naming your works. The titles you give your pieces vary between poetry, romanticism and word play: a statement that is as literal as it is distanced from the works themselves.

BELLET: Placing a title on a work is the same as placing a work on the wall. It already defines it and suggests ways of reading it. The titles supply that, but the ways of reading are often imprecise.

COPELAND: The titles, like your works, often seem temporary, transitory and unstable. Are they simply ways of removing yourself from the picture?

BELLET: Absolutely. Just like that series of self-portraits which are nothing but projections of abstract shadows of my body onto a painting (*Le rideau dans le tableau*, 2009, pp. 107/109). But it's too shallow to suppose that it's merely about stepping back. What excites me is the quest for ways to appear.

1 Michel Philippon: "Paul Valéry, une poétique en poèmes", Bordeaux: Presses universitaires de Bordeaux, 1993.
2 Eliane Radigue's approach is to never appear on stage but to set up all the technical systems in the wings, with the stage containing only the amplifiers.
3 Hans Ulrich Obrist, *Conversation avec Etel Adnan*, Paris: Manuella, 2012, p. 27.

IN THE CORNER OF YOUR MEMORY
2013

APPENDIX

**LE RIDEAU DANS LE TABLEAU
(I–III)**, 2009

Impression jet d'encre sur papier Tintenstrahldruck
auf Papier **Ink-jet print on paper**
I: 35,5 x 29,5 x 2,5 cm; II: 28,5 x 35 x 2,5 cm;
III: 27 x 31 x 2,5 cm
Fond d'art visuel de la ville de Lancy, Genève (I–III)
Sammlung Kunstkredit des Kantons Basel-
Landschaft (I–III)

IDOLE I, 2009
IDOLE II, 2009

Frottage sur papier Frottage auf Papier
Frottage on paper
42 x 29 cm

SUN TWO I, 2009
SUN TWO II, 2009

Frottage sur papier Frottage auf Papier
Frottage on paper
42 x 29 cm

I LOST YOU AGAIN, 2009

Video, 5 min (Edition of 3)
Sammlung Kunstkredit des Kantons Basel-
Landschaft

SÉRENDIPITÉ I, 2010

Papier de soie brûlé Angesengtes Seidenpapier
Burned tissue paper
85 x 160 cm

SANS TITRE SANS ENCRE, 2010

Rouleaux de papier fax (papier thermique) chauffés au
contact d'un radiateur An einem Heizkörper erhitzte
Faxpapierrollen (Thermopapier) **Fax paper rolls
(thermal paper) heated by contact with radiator**
3,95 x 5,1 m
Schweizerisches Architekturmuseum, Basel

BURNING AIR, 2010

Papier de soie doré, brûlé Goldenes Seidenpapier,
verkohlt **Gilt tissue paper, burned**
3,5 x 11 m
Ausstellungsraum Klingental, Basel
Concert by Hidde Van Schie

VESTIGES, 2010
Video, 14 min (Edition of 5)
Sammlung Kunstkredit Basel-Stadt
Musée Jenisch Vevey

BURNING LINE, 2010–2011
Papier de soie brûlé Angesengtes Seidenpapier
Burned tissue paper
Private Collection, Basel

BRÈVE BRAISE, 2011
Papier de soie brûlé Angesengtes Seidenpapier
Burned tissue paper
Ø 2 m

BRILLURE, 2011
Papier de soie brûlé et peinture acrylique Verkohltes Seidenpapier und Acrylfarbe **Burned tissue paper and acrylic paint**
15 x 10 cm

EMPREINTE TACITE I, 2011
EMPREINTE TACITE II, 2011
Photographie (mains de l'artiste, poudre de graphite)
Fotografie (Hände der Künstlerin, Grafitpulver)
Photograph (artist's hands, graphite powder)
70 x 50 cm

 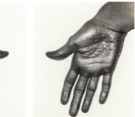

ESCAPE LANDSCAPE, 2011
Video, 9 min (Edition of 5)
Musée Jenisch Vevey

JALOUSIE D'HIER, 2012
Papier de soie doré, froissé Zerknülltes goldenes Seidenpapier **Crumpled gilt tissue paper** &
Tatiana Echeverri Fernandez, *Tired Stone*, 2012
Pierre, corde, poulie et duvet Stein, Seil, Flaschenzug und Duvet **Stone, rope, pully, and duvet**
3,95 x 5,1 m
Hôtel Paravent, tête, Berlin, 2012
Manon Bellet, Tatiana Echeverri Fernandez &
Antonia Low, Installation *in situ*

IMAGERIE DU HASARD, 2011–2012

Réaction thermique sur papier fax mis en contact sur une plaque de métal chauffée au soleil **Thermische Reaktion auf Faxpapier, ausgelöst durch den Kontakt mit einer von der Sonne erwärmten Metallplatte Thermal reaction on fax paper previously placed on a metal plate heated in the sunlight**
Imagerie du hasard V, I, II, III, VII, 2011–2012
Still night, still light, 2011
21 x 15 cm – 32 x 21 cm

 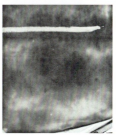

PIPER AT THE GATES OF DAWN, 2012

Papier de soie brûlé, fixé sur le vinyle par l'électricité statique Verkohltes Seidenpapier fixiert mit statischer Elektrizität auf Vinylschallplatte **Burned tissue paper fixed with static electricity on a vinyl record**
Ø 30 cm

TACHE AVEUGLE, 2012

Papier carbone, brûlé Angesengtes Kohlepapier
Burned carbon paper
39 x 29 cm
Private Collection, Italy (pp. 27/29)

PLIS SÛRS, 2012

18 Feuilles de porcelaine 18 Porzellanblätter
18 porcelain sheets
3,8 x 5 m
Private Collection, Basel

SOUS SUR FACE, 2012–2013

Cyanotype Cyanotypie **Cyanotype**
41 x 28,5 cm
Private Collection, Zurich (p. 51)

"CROQUIS DE CHALEUR", 2012–2013

Dessins sur papier thermique réalisé avec clous et objets métalliques chauffés Zeichnungen mit erhitzten Metallnägeln und anderen Objekten auf Thermopapier **Drawings on thermal paper, executed with metal nails and heated objects**
21 x 13 cm – 32 x 21 cm

IN THE CORNER OF YOUR MEMORY, 2012–2013

Revers de films Polaroid périmés, chauffés au soleil In der Sonne erhitzte Rückseiten abgelaufener Polaroidfilme **Sun-heated flipsides of expired Polaroid films**
10 x 8 cm

LAINE DE ROCHE, 2013

Cyanotype Cyanotypie **Cyanotype**
41 x 28,5 cm

BURNING AIR, 2013

Papier de soie, brûlé Seidenpapier, verkohlt **Tissue paper, burned**
Kunsthalle Palazzo, Liestal

ENSEMBLE D'UN ÉCLAT, 2013

Lentille de verre, limaille de fer et aimants Glaslinse, Eisenspäne und Magnete **Glass lens, iron filings, and magnets**
Ø 8 cm

WORKS IN PROGRESS

UNTITLED, 2012
Verre, étiquette transparente Glas, Klarsichtaufkleber
Glass, transparent sticker

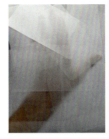  

UNTITLED, 2012
Papier de soie doré Goldenes Seidenpapier
Gilt tissue paper

UNTITLED, 2013
Aimants et limaille de fer sur papier, dimensions variables Magnete und Eisenspäne auf Papier, Grösse variabel **Magnets and iron filings on paper, variable dimensions**

UNTITLED, 2013
Encre de Chine sur papier, tracé à la toupie Tusche auf Papier, Kreiselzeichnung **Ink on paper, gyroscope drawing**
41 x 28,5 cm

UNTITLED, 2013
Aimants et limaille de fer sur papier, dimensions variables Magnete und Eisenspäne auf Papier, Grösse variabel **Magnets and iron filings on paper, variable dimensions**

MANON BELLET

*1979, Vevey
vit et travaille entre Bâle et Berlin
lebt und arbeitet in Basel und Berlin
lives and works in Basel and Berlin
manonbellet.com

FORMATION
AUSBILDUNG
EDUCATION

2000–2002	Cheltenham & Gloucester Art College of Higher Education (Postgraduate Studies), Cheltenham, Gloucestershire, GB
1996–2001	Ecole cantonale d'art du Valais (ECAV), Sierre, CH

RÉSIDENCES
AUSLANDAUFENTHALTE
RESIDENCIES

2012	Cité des Arts, Paris, F (iaab Basel)
2007	Berlin, D (iaab Basel)
2005	Centre for Contemporary Art, Warszawa, PL (iaab Basel)
2003	Werkraum Warteck PP, Basel, CH

PRIX ET BOURSES
STIPENDIEN
SCHOLARSHIPS

2012	Cahiers d'Artistes, Pro Helvetia, CH
2011	Nerinum Fondation, Buenos Aires, AR
2007	Fondation Irène Reymond, Lausanne, CH
2006	Kunstkredit Basel-Stadt, Basel, CH
	Alexander Clavel Stiftung, Riehen, CH

EXPOSITIONS PERSONNELLES
EINZELAUSSTELLUNGEN
SOLO EXHIBITIONS

2013–2014	*Manon Bellet. L'onde d'une ombre,* Kunstmuseum Solothurn & Musée Jenisch Vevey, CH
2010	*Double exposure,* in coll. with Pedro Barateiro, Rua Madalena Project, Lisboa, P
2007	*Ombrée,* Lodypop, Basel, CH

EXPOSITIONS COLLECTIVES (SÉLECTION)
GRUPPENAUSSTELLUNGEN (AUSWAHL)
GROUP EXHIBITIONS (SELECTION)

2014 12ème Triennale Bex et Arts, CH

2013 *Trait Papier*, Kunsthalle Palazzo, Liestal & Musée d'art contemporain de Yverdon-les-Bains, CH
Summershow, GRIFFIN'S, Berlin, D
Time, OSLO 10, Basel, CH
Talk to the Hand, Sprechende Fäuste, Patentierte Gesten, Helmhaus Zürich, CH
Nouvelles Vagues, Galerie Isabelle Gounod, Paris, in coll. with Palais de Tokyo, Paris, F

2012 *Prix Irène Reymond, Lauréats 2006–2011,* Musée d'art de Pully, CH
Death Can Dance, TOWNHOUSE, Zürich, CH
Hôtel Paravent, tête, Berlin, D

2011 *Autofokus* {and meantime belongs to becoming}, General Public, Berlin, D
ERNTE 11, Kunstankäufe 2010 des Kantons Basel-Landschaft, Kunsthaus Baselland, CH
Traceable, Galleria Zak, Siena, I

2010 Werkbeiträge Kunstkredit Basel-Stadt, Schweizerisches Architekturmuseum, Basel, CH
Yesterday Will Be Better – Mit der Erinnerung in die Zukunft, Aargauer Kunsthaus, Aarau, CH
F+, Ausstellungsraum Klingental, Basel, CH
Kunstsammlung Hoffmann-La Roche, Basel, CH
Pas du jeu, le Manoir, Martigny, CH
Casting, Galerie Visite ma tente, Berlin, D

2009 *Choice* (TRABANT #14), in coll. with iaab & Vrits, Ausstellungsraum Klingental, Basel, CH
Regionale 10, Kunsthaus Baselland, CH
Des mondes voisins, Galerie Gisèle Linder, Basel, CH

2008 *Line (cross the),* Villa Bernasconi, Genève, CH
Young and Beautiful – 10 Jahre Kunst Raum Riehen, Kunst Raum Riehen, CH
Papier, Galerie Gisèle Linder, Basel, CH

2007 *Accrochage* [Vaud 2007], Espace Arlaud, Lausanne, CH
Zeichnungen, Galerie Gisèle Linder, Basel, CH

2005 Projektraum M 54, Basel, CH
Excentricities, Zentrum für Kulturproduktion, Bern, CH

2004 *Regionale 5,* Kunst Raum Riehen, CH & Kunstverein Freiburg i. Br., D
Accrochage [Vaud 2004], Musée cantonal des Beaux-Arts de Lausanne, CH

2003 *Regionale 4,* Kunsthalle Basel, CH

AUTRES PROJETS (SÉLECTION)
WEITERE PROJEKTE (AUSWAHL)
FURTHER PROJECTS (SELECTION)

2009 *Diorigine,* Bblackboxx, Basel, CH
2008–2009 *Manerie,* in coll. with Luis Garey (Choreography), Florencia Vecino (Dance), Internationales Musikfestival B. Martinu, Voltahalle, Basel, CH & El portòn de Sanchez, Buenos Aires, AR
2007 *Expansion sonore,* SHIFT – Festival der elektronischen Künste, Basel, CH
2005 *Dancing,* Performance in coll. with Zamek Ujazdowski, Centre for Contemporary Art, Warszawa, PL
2003 VIPER, Internationales Festival für Film, Video und neue Medien, Basel, CH

PUBLICATION
PUBLIKATION
PUBLICATION

2013 *Cahiers d'Artistes,* Pro Helvetia, Luzern/Poschiavo: Edizioni Periferia, 2013 (Text: Julie Enckell Julliard).

TEXTES (SÉLECTION)
TEXTE (AUSWAHL)
TEXTS (SELECTION)

Nouvelles Vagues, le Magazine du Palais de Tokyo, été 2013, exh. cat., n°7.1/2, 2013, 242–245.

« Expérience de carnets », *Le carnet de recherches,* numéro spécial, Roven n°9, printemps-été 2013, 98–103.

Julie Enckell Julliard, « Papier solo », *Trait Papier, un essai sur le dessin contemporain,* exh. cat., Musée des beaux-arts de La Chaux-de-Fonds, Genève : Coédition L'Apage & Atrabile, 2012, 88–99.

Daniel Morgenthaler, « Vestiges », *Yesterday Will Be Better – Mit der Erinnerung in die Zukunft,* exh. cat., Aargauer Kunsthaus, Aarau, Bielefeld: Kerber, 2010, 72–75.

COLLECTIONS PUBLIQUES
WERKE IN ÖFFENTLICHEN SAMMLUNGEN
WORKS IN PUBLIC COLLECTIONS

Fonds d'art visuel de la ville de Lancy, Genève, CH
Kunstkredit Basel-Landschaft, Basel, CH
Kunstkredit Basel-Stadt, Basel, CH
Kunstsammlung Hoffmann-La Roche, Basel, CH
Musée Jenisch Vevey, CH

AUTOREN

PATRICIA BIEDER (*1985) ist seit 2012 wissenschaftliche Assistentin im Kunstmuseum Solothurn. Studium der Englischen Literaturwissenschaften und Kunstgeschichte in Bern und Cardiff (UK). 2007–2008 Praktikum in der Gemäldegalerie Alte Meister, Dresden. Erste Katalogtexte im Bereich der zeitgenössischen Schweizer Kunst (Kathrin Borer, Klodin Erb, Susan Hodel, Giacomo Santiago Rogado u.a.).

MATHIEU COPELAND (*1977), Studium am Goldsmith College in London bis 2003. Freischaffender Kurator zahlreicher Ausstellungen, darunter Co-Kuration von *VIDES, Une Rétrospective* im Centre Pompidou Paris und in der Kunsthalle Bern. Initiator der Ausstellungs-Serien *Exposition parlée* und *Exposition à être lue*. 2013 hat er die monographischen Ausstellungen von Gustav Metzger im Musée d'art contemporain in Lyon sowie von Phill Niblock im Centre d'art Circuit und im Musée de l'Elysée in Lausanne kuratiert. Er unterrichtet an der Haute Ecole d'Art et de Design (HEAD) in Genf und hat Lehraufträge an verschiedenen Universitäten und Kunsthochschulen.

JULIE ENCKELL JULLIARD (*1974), promovierte 2004 und absolvierte anschliessend den Postgraduate-Lehrgang an der HEAD in Genf mit den Schwerpunkten Kritik, kuratorische Fragen und Cyber-Medien. Seit 2013 Direktorin des Musée Jenisch Vevey, zuvor von 2007 bis 2012 Konservatorin für moderne und zeitgenössische Kunst im Musée Jenisch Vevey. Sie war wissenschaftliche Kuratorin mehrerer Ausstellungen zeitgenössischer Kunstschaffender, darunter Silvia Buonvicini, Balthasar Burkhard, Rudy Decelière, Alain Huck, Denis Savary und Ante Timmermans. 2010–2011 hat sie die Ausstellung *Voici un dessin suisse* kuratiert. Zahlreiche Publikationen zur zeitgenössischen Kunst, der Ausstellungsgeschichte der Zeichnung oder des Gebrauchs des Papiers in der zeitgenössischen Kunst.

STÉPHANIE SERRA (*1985) ist seit 2013 stellvertretende Kuratorin für zeitgenössische Kunst im Musée Jenisch Vevey und Vor-Doktorandin an der HEAD in Genf. Sie interessiert sich für die Verbindung zwischen den Städten und der Produktion des Imaginären quer durch Brasilien, die Türkei und Basel, die sie im Rahmen einer Forschungsarbeit zwischen 2009 und 2010 an der Universität Bocconi in Mailand untersuchte, und vertieft sich seit 2011 in die junge Schweizer Kunstszene.

AUTEURS

PATRICIA BIEDER (*1985) est collaboratrice scientifique au Musée des Beaux-Arts de Soleure depuis 2012. Elle a étudié la littérature anglaise et l'histoire de l'art à Berne et à Cardiff (Royaume-Uni). En 2007–2008 elle était stagiaire à la galerie de peinture Alte Meister de Dresde. Ses premiers écrits portent sur Kathrin Borer, Klodin Erb, Susan Hodel, entre autres.

MATHIEU COPELAND (*1977) a obtenu le diplôme du Goldsmith College de Londres en 2003. Curateur indépendant, il a co-organisé l'exposition *VIDES, Une Rétrospective* au Centre Pompidou Paris et à la Kunsthalle de Berne. Il a organisé de nombreuses expositions et initié les séries d'*Exposition parlée,* et d'*Exposition à être lue*. En 2013, il est commissaire de l'exposition monographique de Gustav Metzger au Musée d'art contemporain de Lyon, ainsi que de l'exposition Phill Niblock au Centre d'art Circuit et au Musée de l'Elysée à Lausanne. Il enseigne à la HEAD – Haute Ecole d'Art et de Design de Genève, et intervient dans de nombreuses universités et écoles d'arts.

JULIE ENCKELL JULLIARD (*1974), auteur d'une thèse de doctorat en 2004, elle a obtenu un diplôme postgrade de la HEAD dans le cadre du pôle Critique, Curatorial et Cybermédia. Conservatrice Art moderne et contemporain au Musée Jenisch Vevey entre 2007 et 2012, elle dirige le musée depuis 2013. Elle a assuré le commissariat de plusieurs expositions dont celles de Silvia Buonvicini, Balthasar Burkhard, Rudy Decelière, Alain Huck, Denis Savary et Ante Timmermans. En 2010–2011, elle a organisé l'exposition *Voici un dessin suisse*. Elle est aussi l'auteur d'une quarantaine d'écrits, allant des études monographiques à l'histoire des expositions de dessin ou l'usage du papier dans l'art contemporain.

STÉPHANIE SERRA (*1985), conservatrice adjointe Art contemporain au Musée Jenisch Vevey depuis 2013 et pré-doctorante à la HEAD, s'intéresse au lien entre les villes et la production d'imaginaires au travers d'un projet de recherche transversal au Brésil, en Turquie et à Bâle, mené entre 2009 et 2010 à l'Université Bocconi de Milan, et approfondit depuis 2011 la scène artistique suisse émergente.

Diese Publikation erscheint anlässlich der Einzelausstellung
Cet ouvrage paraît à l'occasion de l'exposition de

Manon Bellet. L'onde d'une ombre

Kunstmuseum Solothurn
29.11.13 – 09.02.14

Musée Jenisch Vevey
21.03.14 – 01.06.14

PUBLIKATION
PUBLICATION
Projektleitung Direction du projet :
Patricia Bieder, Julie Enckell Julliard
Redaktionelle Koordination Coordination éditoriale :
Patricia Bieder
Redaktion Rédaction :
Patricia Bieder, Julie Enckell Julliard, Stéphanie Serra
Texte Textes :
Patricia Bieder, Mathieu Copeland, Julie Enckell Julliard, Stéphanie Serra
Übersetzungen Traductions :
Fiona Elliott (Patricia Bieder), Suzanne Schmidt
(S. pp. 115–119), Geoffrey Spearing (Mathieu Copeland, Julie Enckell Julliard, Stéphanie Serra)
Verlagslektorat Relecture :
Axel Lapp
Grafische Gestaltung Conception graphique :
Anja Lutz // Book Design, Berlin
Gesamtherstellung Impression :
DZA Druckerei zu Altenburg GmbH, Altenburg

© 2013 The Green Box, the artist, authors and photographers

ISBN 978-3-941644-62-5

Verlag Maison d'édition :
The Green Box
Kunst Editionen, Berlin
www.thegreenbox.net

FOTONACHWEIS
CRÉDITS PHOTOGRAPHIQUES
Viktor Kolibàl: S. pp. 4, 18, 20, 21, 22, 41, 58, 59, 60, 99, 100, 101, 102, 104, 105, 107, 109
Meinrad Hofer: S. p. 19
Alle anderen Aufnahmen Toutes les autres images :
Manon Bellet

Cover: Empreinte Tacite II, 2011

Die Künstlerin dankt besonders L'artiste souhaite remercier tout particulièrement :
Patricia Bieder, Christoph Vögele, Julie Enckell Julliard, Stéphanie Serra, Mathieu Copeland, Anja Lutz, Erik Kiesewetter, Christian Müller, Til Frentzel, Jürg Dreier

Mit herzlichem Dank auch an Nous tenons aussi à remercier :
Gisèle Linder, Matthias Marx (Mitsubishi HiTec Paper Europe GmbH), Daniel Morgenthaler, Letizia Schubiger, Madeleine Schuppli, Karine Tissot, Team Kunstmuseum Solothurn, équipe du Musée Jenisch Vevey

Mit grosszügiger Unterstützung Avec le généreux soutien :

AUSSTELLUNG IM KUNSTMUSEUM SOLOTHURN

Konzept der Ausstellung: Manon Bellet und Patricia Bieder

Konservator: Christoph Vögele
Wissenschaftliche Assistentin: Patricia Bieder
Sekretariat: Christine Kobel
Verwaltung: Stefan Gschwind
Registrar: Christian Müller
Ausstellungstechnik: Til Frentzel, Jürg Dreier, Christian Müller
Museumspädagogik: Claudia Leimer und Regula Straumann
Aufsicht: Diana Brunner, Ursy Caduff, Jürg Dreier, Esther Eggenschwiler, Jacqueline Kummli, Madeleine Salzmann Lischer

EXPOSITION AU MUSÉE JENISCH VEVEY

Concept de l'exposition: Manon Bellet
Commissariat de l'exposition: Julie Enckell Julliard, assistée de Stéphanie Serra

Direction: Julie Enckell Julliard
Conservatrice Cabinet cantonal des estampes et Direction adjointe: Laurence Schmidlin
Conservatrice adjointe Art contemporain: Stéphanie Serra
Conservatrice adjointe Cabinet cantonal des estampes: Camille Jaquier
Conservatrice adjointe Art moderne: Emmanuelle Neukomm
Régie des oeuvres: Justine Dufour
Administration générale et comptabilité: Bernadette Jobin, Isabelle Richoz
Presse, communication, web: Fabienne Aellen, Marion Lafarge
Réception et boutique: Marion Lafarge, Arcelia Hauert
Vernissages: Agnes Duboux
Equipe technique: Michel Cap, Dominique Gigante
Technicien de maintenance, Sécurité: Fabian Z'Graggen, J.D. Frachebaud

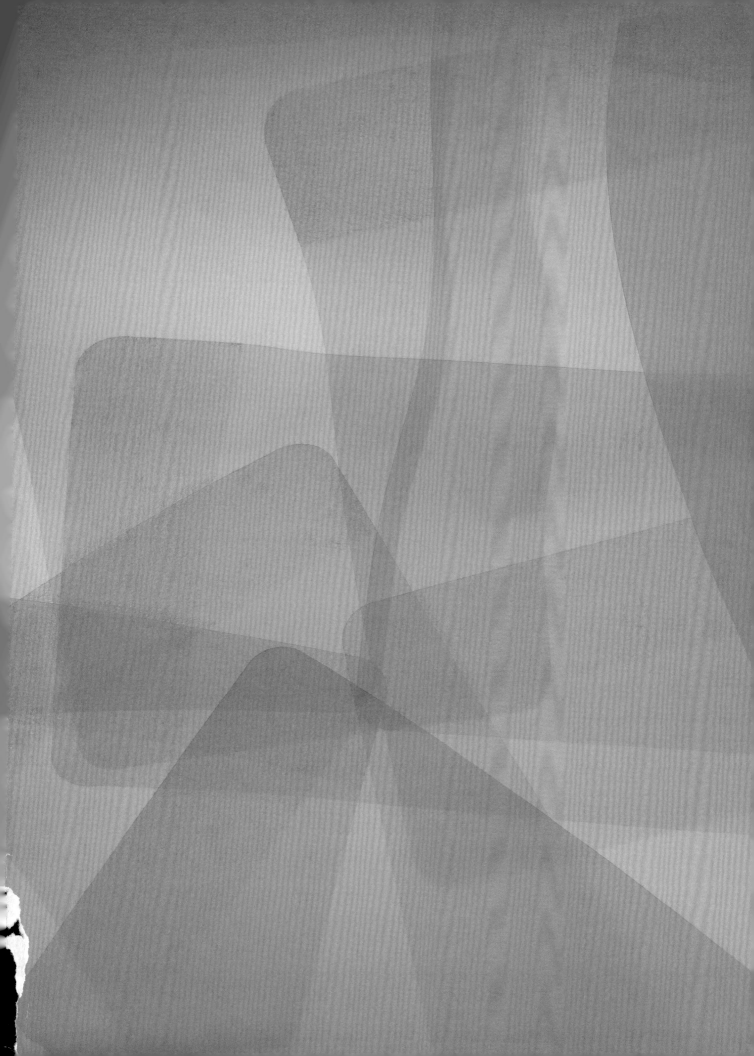